Engendering
#BlackGirlJoy

Venus E. Evans-Winters
Series Editor

Vol. 1

The Urban Girls series is part of the Peter Lang Education list.
Every volume is peer reviewed and meets
the highest quality standards for content and production.

PETER LANG
New York • Bern • Berlin
Brussels • Vienna • Oxford • Warsaw

Monique Lane

Engendering #BlackGirlJoy

How to Cultivate Empowered Identities and Educational Persistence in Struggling Schools

Foreword by Bettina Love

PETER LANG
New York • Bern • Berlin
Brussels • Vienna • Oxford • Warsaw

Library of Congress Cataloging-in-Publication Data

Names: Lane, Monique, author.
Title: Engendering #blackgirljoy: how to cultivate empowered identities and educational persistence in struggling schools/ Monique Lane; foreword by Bettina Love.
Description: New York: Peter Lang, 2021.
Series: Urban girls; v. 1
ISSN 2470-122X (print) | ISSN 2470-1211 (online)
Includes bibliographical references and index.
Identifiers: LCCN 2018023787 | ISBN 978-1-4331-5879-7 (hardback)
ISBN 978-1-4331-5878-0 (paperback) | ISBN 978-1-4331-5880-3 (ebook pdf)
ISBN 978-1-4331-5881-0 (epub)
Subjects: LCSH: African American girls—Education (Secondary)—Social aspects—United States. | Urban schools—Social aspects—United States. | Feminism and education—United States. | Culturally relevant pedagogy—United States.
Classification: LCC LC2779 .L36 | DDC 371.829/96073—dc23
LC record available at https://lccn.loc.gov/2018023787
DOI 10.3726/b17317

Bibliographic information published by **Die Deutsche Nationalbibliothek**.
Die Deutsche Nationalbibliothek lists this publication in the "Deutsche Nationalbibliografie"; detailed bibliographic data are available on the Internet at http://dnb.d-nb.de/.

Cover design and interior illustrations by Nimah Gobir

© 2021 Peter Lang Publishing, Inc., New York
80 Broad Street, 5th floor, New York, NY 10004
www.peterlang.com

To my delicious littles, Lena and Raj,
who have enriched my life.
Thank you for keeping me humble, patient,
and centered.
I pray that the Universe blesses you with a
fiery and unyielding passion
to pursue your wildest dreams.
And teachers who value your humanity.

Table of Contents

Foreword

Children of color in America are simultaneously the most studied and the most underserved. And when they are studied, they are studied from a deficit approach. This scholarship is violent and has produced countless teachers who believe that the identities of young Black girls are unwanted in the classroom and disruptive to the very fabric of schooling. For this reason, we need new playbooks based on new research. We need Black women researchers who were once little Black girls because we can and must tell our own stories, contextualize our own pain, and never take our eyes off the prize of remembering and living Black joy.

If you are picking up this book, you already know that Black girls are special. Black girls possess a joy that is unmatched and needed in all communities, but especially where Black girls live. Justice cannot happen without joy: justice and Black girls are a dual necessity. For educators to understand #BlackGirlJoy and see it as an essential lever for educational justice, teachers must study #BlackGirlJoy. We must dig into the historical, navigational, spiritual, and pedagogical approaches of Black girls to first, marvel in their magic, then begin to shift the structure of schooling to embody #BlackGirlJoy, which means spaces that are gender affirming, unapologetically Black, intergenerational, and communal. A #BlackGirlJoy school model is what schools should be, but as Monique writes, "They Keep Stealin' Our Joy." They steal our joy with standardized testing, stale curriculum, zero tolerance policies, and expelling and suspending Black girls for being Black girls.

Engendering #BlackGirlJoy: How to Cultivate Empowered Identities and Educational Persistence in Struggling Schools shows us how to marvel at Black girls' self-discovery, voice, and Blackness through the lens of Black feminism. As a Black feminist, I see Monique's work as an urgent request to think about Black girls in ways that push our understanding of their lives by giving them the space to self-define: a needed, paradigm shifting approach. The voices of Black girls within the pages of this book are critical, powerful, bold, and honest about the complex work of Black life as a Black girl. I am honored that Monique asked me to write the foreword of this powerful book. I hope that you will go on this journey with her to bring the joy of Black girls not only into our schools, but into our world. We need it more than we will ever know.

Bettina L. Love
Atlanta, GA

Acknowledgements

Conducting this inquiry and completing this book project were equal parts terrific and terrifying. I am indebted to the community of folks who cheered me on along the way.

This book would not be possible without Dr. V—Venus Evans-Winters—the Urban Girls series editor and big sister in my head. I appreciate the platforms that you have offered to illuminate my work. I have been privileged to watch and learn from how you *do* academia. As a powerful scholar and mentor to countless young intellectuals, you are an ambitious model to follow! Also, I express my gratitude to the folks at Peter Lang Publishing. Patricia Mulrane Clayton, thank you for trusting in the creative direction of this project, and for your patience as it evolved.

I offer tremendous appreciation to Bettina Love. You have blessed this book with a *fire* foreword that compels readers to come along for the ride. Thank you for accepting my invitation to participate in this project. Your brilliance is luminous, and I am grateful for your generosity.

Also, I want to recognize my mentors—a group of esteemed colleagues who have guided me, dating back to graduate school. I could not have completed this endeavor without the insights and skillful encouragement of Drs. Patrick Camangian, Tyrone Howard, Ernest Morrell, and Yolanda Sealey-Ruiz. I also want to thank Drs. Thomas Philip, Kimberly Gomez, and Peter McClaren. You each read parts of this book in some form. Thank you for pushing me to dig deeper, "be awesomer," and take up more space in the academy.

And I would be remiss if I did not thank my *sista scholar homegurls*! Drs. Ifeoma Amah, Karisa Peer, and Crystal Belle reminded me time and again to prioritize community and self-care throughout this process. I am deeply grateful for the meet-ups, phone calls, video chats, and occasional check-ins via text messaging.

To my colleagues at Saint Mary's College of California and the faculty in the Leadership Department: thank you for granting me grace while I birthed a baby and a book in the same year.

Nimah Gobir, your artistic talents and creativity elevated my words and renewed the spirit of the book. You nailed it! Thanks for your labor and your time.

I also want to offer an enormous thank you to my editor, Jordan Beltran Gonzales. With your care, professionalism, and expertise—we nurtured this book to completion. Your enthusiasm for this project was invaluable.

I am extraordinarily lucky to have had the support of my family while I wrote this book. To my dearly departed parents, I will never take for granted your interest in my educational pursuits and your unyielding confidence in my abilities. I look forward to reading this entire book to you, *aloud*, when I meet you on the other side! To my phenomenal stepparents, Jake and Lesbia Ross, and the Phillips/Richardson and Laud families—I am indebted to you for holding me up when my foundation was shaky.

To my "ride or die" sisters and BFF—Jynne Ross, Sparkale Ross, and Kashana Moncrief-Williams—your belief in my "magic" is tenacious. You have journeyed with me through graduate school, a postdoctoral fellowship, two cross-country moves, a couple of children, and my trials and triumphs as a faculty member. Thank you for loving me through the rainbows and the storms. And, for your uncanny ability to recite old school Black film quotes randomly in conversation. You each made me smile when finishing this book preoccupied my life.

Additionally, I offer gratitude to my babies, Lena and Raj. Your love kept me buoyed when completing this book felt impossible. You have gifted me with a deeper sense of awareness and compassion. I am a better teacher, scholar, and human being because of you.

I want to shout out, *from the rooftop*, my husband and life partner, Nikhil Laud. For the past 16 years, you have supported me more than any other person on the planet. Thank you for pushing me outside of my comfort zone, believing in my capacity for greatness, and for "keeping the tiny humans alive" while mama grinds! I am grateful for your sacrifices. Thank you for your devotion to our family. I love you, infinitely.

Amongst the support mentioned above, the King High School community impacted this project most profoundly. To the staff, teachers, and administrators: I have a special place in my heart for the folks who showed up every day, with earnest intentions, to "do right" by Black and Brown children. To the young people who I encountered inside and outside of my classroom, thank you for challenging and inspiring me. Our time together ignited my Black feminist sensibility—which has shaped the trajectory of my personal and professional lives.

Lastly, I want to thank *my girls*. I vividly recall the hectic pace at King High School, and I was often embroiled in the chaos of teaching. However, your energy was a motivating force, and our conversations reified my purpose. I am honored that you have entrusted me with your stories. Moreover, I sincerely appreciate the opportunity to celebrate your humanity and amplify your wisdom through this book. In all of your future endeavors, please remember to center *joy*. Know that you are infused with a divine light, and you possess the power to change the world. I love each of you to the moon and back! I will forever rep' "sisterhood, solidarity, and self-love"!

I am from early mornings and mama singin' the blues.
From kickbacks and cadillacs to breakin' all the rules.
Where I'm from, crooked cops make pit stops on boulevards of despair.
Police brutality is a grim reality – but I guess it ain't supposed to be fair.

Where I'm from, soldiers in camouflage pump black fists high, with pride.
The legacy of Malcolm and Assata behind every stride.
Revolution's the only solution, at least that's what they say.
Steady tryin' to break the cycle of self-hate impairing shorties around the way.

Cuz' see, I'm from 'Aye aye baby what's yo' name?'
Bloodshot eyes gazing at me from behind, and he know he got game!
From bad-mouthed ballers, gold chains heavy like steel.
They are Kings in disguise. Humanity compromised. Genius concealed.

I am from Queens to doodoo mamas, flips, and two-bit whores.
And when we at school they call us fools, cuz' the Black woman is deplored.
Where I'm from, feminism is synonymous with lesbian or bitch.
But I'd rather be that, than a f*$#! door mat, and you can get wit' it or be dismissed.

See, I'm from a place u can't replicate,
Ain't no science producing a clone.
And although it's hood and we're misunderstood,
This is the place I call home.

~Monique Lane

Chapter One

Introduction

Hindsight Is 20/20

As an education professor and former high school English teacher, I endorse the notion that all practice is theory-driven. What teachers *do* in the classroom is undeniably informed by what they *believe*. Accordingly, to support Teacher Leaders in their pursuit to become transformative educators, my graduate studies program begins with a class that challenges students to use a critical lens as they investigate the personal beliefs that guide their practice. As the instructor of the inaugural course, I required graduate students to discuss how their multiple identities (e.g., race, gender, sexual orientation, religion, class, and ability) were situated within community and school contexts and how interactions at those sites have influenced candidates' sense of self and their Teacher Leader practice. In the past, I have selected autoethnography as the method to conduct these self-explorations. Anchoring personal narratives in a socio-political frame, autoethnographies (a) examine the alienating effects of society, (b) explore connections within and across cultures, and (c) strategize for hope and social change (Carey-Webb, 2001).

When Master of Arts Degree candidates re-tell their narratives as politicized beings, these learners evolve immensely as they sharpen their understandings of the ties between their personal beliefs and their professional practice. Moreover, shining a light on educators' ideological postures—and the inherent power, privilege, and biases that individuals bring into the classroom—is the first step toward cultivating equity-minded practitioners who lead with intention.

It is natural for human beings to trust the verisimilitude of personal experience. Hence, it is ambitious and risky to ask teachers to disrupt their cultural paradigms and challenge processes of domination. In my experience, the most insightful examinations of oneself through critical autoethnography frequently emerge when graduate students feel *safe* enough to examine their personal stories and various intersections of their identities from a new perspective. Recognizing the difficulty of fostering a classroom climate that promotes trust and vulnerability between instructors and students in institutions of higher education, I initiate the process of putting our subjective lenses "on blast," and I model the self-reflexivity that I expect from teachers. Each year, as I prepare to present an autoethnography centered on my educational trajectory, I grapple with the fear of inviting curious strangers into the intimate details of my youth, which I interpret within a broader sociocultural context. As a Black woman scholar at a predominantly White institution (PWI), moreover, I routinely negotiate racism and gender discrimination in the classroom (e.g., racial micro-aggressions, lack of respect, tokenism, and pushback on anti-racist curriculum). In light of my precarious position, sharing my lived experience and calling out oppressive power structures—in front of an audience of predominantly White students, no less—has the inevitable potential to jeopardize my status as the instructor of the course. However, as someone who embodies the ethic of risk-taking that is fundamental to Black Feminist pedagogical praxis (Beauboeuf-Lafontant, 2002), I regularly jeopardize my comfort levels, opting to engage graduate students in difficult conversations that lead to their social and intellectual maturation. Wavering between audacity and apprehension, I reveal my cultural narrative on the first day of each class, optimistic that the unquantifiable benefits of sharing my story outweigh the apparent risks.

As I stand before education graduate students and bare my truth, I reflect on the magic and misfortune of my selfhood and breathe new life into my narrative. Using autoethnographic introspection, I elucidate my trajectory from an urban Black girl learner—awkwardly ensconced in a matrix of systemic disadvantage—to an educational scholar researching the schooling experiences of African American youth similar to my younger self. Periodically, I introduce new people and events into the story; nevertheless, the same themes emerge. Variations of racialized sexist oppression, sexual harassment, hegemonic violence, and girlhood rebellion have surfaced in each presentation of my testimony. Since it is impractical to expose the linear span of my P–12 and postsecondary education in a 20-minute presentation, I center the discussion on one of the most formative fragments of my lifetime of schooling: my tenure as a high school student.

In grades nine through twelve, I attended a large, academically and materially under-resourced public high school in South Los Angeles. During those four years, I routinely encountered instances in which teachers, administrators, and classmates mercilessly attacked one or more dimensions of my identity. In one typical day, I occupied multiple spaces—each commingling race, class, and gender politics. In my classes, well-meaning yet misguided educators trivialized my intelligence. In the hallways, teenage boys (and the occasional male teacher) ogled and assaulted my maturing brown body via sexist epithets. Moreover, the ubiquity of reductive images of low-income African American women in the media—that positioned us as icons of cultural deviation and pathology—had me convinced that I was a social leper, linked to a group of naturally inferior people. Despite my efforts at negotiating these offenses—a front of indifference, mean-muggin', and the seldom quick-witted counterattack—each interaction left an imprint of shame on my dignity, and the collective effect was a powerful strike against my humanity.

Struggling to cope with the distress of school-induced trauma and lacking a formal space to critically analyze these experiences, I bore my stigma of shame in silence. Not only did my college prep courses for highly gifted students traditionally disregard oppressive social conditions, but these classes often reinforced them through curricula that valorized White middle-class norms. As such, I was young, gifted, and *deeply embattled*. There was, however, a glimmer of hope. In my senior year, I received acceptance to the University of California, Los Angeles (UCLA) and I eagerly awaited the challenges and opportunities that college would present. After encountering feminist and critical race theories in my undergraduate education courses, I recognized the complex ways in which the social and academic identities of students of color are co-constructed and mediated within the schooling context, as well as how this process influences the educational outcomes of historically underserved youth. This epiphany led me into teaching, and I sought to become the type of educator I wished I had had in high school.

After earning my bachelor's degree from UCLA, I returned to my alma mater and taught high school English for five years. As a young practitioner in my early 20s, the beauty and the terror of my life history as a Black girl and woman had settled deep into my consciousness. Armed with an intimate understanding of the factors that jeopardized marginalized students' educational resilience, I willfully incorporated feminist epistemologies, digital technologies, and critical media literacy as tools to affirm students' diverse cultural heritages and disrupt social stressors that impeded their ability to thrive as learners and human beings. In fact, I readily discussed the barriers I faced as an adolescent and co-constructed resistance strategies alongside my teenage scholars to enrich our collective capacity for healing. It was in those shared moments of vulnerability that we accessed the temporal spaces of agency and possibility, and I connected most with the young people whom I had the pleasure of teaching.

In retrospect, I have completed 15 orbits around the sun since my first day as a classroom teacher. As a college professor, I now understand—perhaps more than ever—how contesting normative constructions of identity is a critical site of (re)humanization that is essential to nurture learners of all ages. Accordingly, the autoethnography remains a staple in my arsenal of community-building activities with in-service teachers, and I introduce the assignment during the first class session of each academic year. Moreover, by engaging a retrospective gaze and articulating the educational toxins that preoccupied me as an adolescent, I have discovered that as a woman of color and former urban Black girl, I share a complex identity that is "distinct from, yet inclusive of the world around me" (hooks, 1996, xi).

They Keep Stealin' Our Joy

After numerous years of sense-making through autoethnographic examinations, I have a refined understanding of how the accretions of trauma that I encountered throughout my educational journey have informed my personal development. In hindsight, I have also come to realize that the challenges I navigated as a Black girl learner are neither new nor uncommon. My personal battles in school are consistent with a larger body of experiences among Black girl adolescents throughout the nation. With the turn of the twenty-first century, the continuing struggle for young Black women's liberation has become increasingly volatile, due in part to the ceaseless flow of racialized misogyny in hip-hop and popular culture. As Black feminist critic Patricia Hill Collins (2000) has intimated, the prevailing philosophy of the slave era sparked the evolution of various interrelated, controlling images of Black womanhood. Socially constructed characterizations of African American women—as mammies, matriarchs, welfare recipients, and hot mommas—"reflects the dominant group's interest in maintaining Black women's subordination" and upholds White supremacy (Collins, 2000, p. 72). Likewise, Bettina Love's (2017) recent scholarship exposes how Black women and girl learners across the United States—including cisgender, queer, and transgender youth—continue to negotiate normative expressions of femininity that are propagated by the White middle class. Love's counter-cultural reading of the term *ratchet*—a contemporary disreputable media narrative that depicts low-income Black women and girls as aggressive, irresponsible, and anti-intellectual—complicates education stakeholders' understandings of these students' agency and resilience as they challenge the aesthetics of respectability both inside and outside of the schooling context.

As traditional education offers a limited critical analysis of Black women's shifting social struggles, standardized curricula remain disengaging and consequently undermine the development of Black girl learners' transformative agency in classroom spaces. Education scholars have produced a number of important studies examining the role of standardized curriculums on the self-perception and academic well-being of young Black women students (Fordham, 1996; Power-Carter, 2007). Most of this work tends to focus on interrogating the differential ways in which Black girl learners navigate conventional schooling environments, with a limited discussion of practical and effective methods of academic instruction that reconcile the marginalization that these learners experience. Nonetheless, previous scholarship reifies the evaded notion that public schools are failing young Black women. Academic literature examining declining high school graduation rates, urban Black girl resiliency, and disparate life outcomes among these learners substantiate this claim. African American girl learners are typically (a) excluded from advanced placement (AP) and college preparatory courses, (b) less likely to graduate from high school on time, (c) overrepresented in community colleges, and (d) register with and matriculate from four-year institutions at lower rates than other racialized women (Archer-Banks & Behar-Horenstein, 2012; Evans-Winters, 2011; The NAACP Legal Defense and Educational Fund & The National Women's Law Center, 2014). Alarmingly, the lack of parity that persists between the overall educational attainment of African American women and girls and their young women counterparts is reflected in Black women's subjugated labor positions and resulting racial and spatial isolation in urban ghettos.

The bleak educational and socio-political landscape depicted above poignantly underscores the need for schooling interventions that challenge rather than perpetuate the liminal space in which society positions Black girls. To note, numerous scholars have well-theorized how today's schools—in their efforts to mold students into future workers that help U.S. companies compete in a global economy—jettison the cultural assets, skills, and intellectual practices that racially and linguistically diverse learners bring into the classroom. The rationale that education stakeholders have exploited to legitimize what researcher Angela Valenzuela (1999) calls *subtractive schooling* is that low-income and non-white students are bereft of the necessary social knowledge, cognitive abilities, and cultural capital due to their social class and racial background (Bourdieu & Passeron, 1977). Such thinking has emboldened countless P–12 practitioners to enact irresponsible curricular and instructional decisions that primarily focus on preparing students for high-stakes testing and adapting youth to structures of social domination. Extensive literature promotes culturally affirming pedagogies, which teaches *to and through* the strengths of students from non-dominant backgrounds (Gay, 2000). However, these methods are scarcely employed in U.S. schools and are especially difficult to sustain in institutions that are low-functioning due to high teacher and administrative turnover, scripted curriculum, limited academic resources, and heightened student disengagement.

Comparable to what I encountered as an adolescent, twenty-first century schools struggle to equip learners—and Black girls, specifically—to locate, analyze, heal from, and ultimately thrive through the suffering they experience inside and outside of academic contexts. In fact, after teaching and mentoring African American young women for roughly 15 years, I have thought long and hard about how schools violently deplete the *joy* from Black girls' spirits. Brittney Cooper's (2018) scholarship provides the perfect introduction into an examination of #BlackGirlJoy, a concept that I elucidate in this book. Cooper contends that for Black women, *joy* "arises from an internal clarity about our purpose" (p. 274). Contrary to happiness, which is predicated on external circumstances, #BlackGirlJoy is tied to Black women and girls' conscious unfolding—namely, the journey to self-define and evolve—in the face of abundant systemic injustices. Day after day, African American girls enter schools with a strong sense of cultural pride and a distinctive standpoint gifted by maternal elders in their families and communities (e.g., grandmothers, mothers, aunts, older sisters, play cousins, and community othermothers; Collins, 2000). However, when these youth cross the threshold into P–12 classrooms, this specialized knowledge is suppressed by practitioners' malignant disregard for the worldviews and social literacies that African American women have historically relied on to survive in oppressive locations. In order to alleviate Black girls' persistent disenfranchisement and disparate school outcomes, it is imperative that education stakeholders designate spaces within schools to resurrect the #BlackGirlJoy that is necessary to combat social inequities and restore these learners' well-being.

The Purpose of the Book

Anchored in the immeasurable depths of school-related stressors, young Black women are knee-deep in a struggle to preserve their humanity. Hence, an urgent challenge for education practitioners and researchers is to identify the pedagogical practices that foster #BlackGirlJoy, an emotionally and psychologically protective state that sustains African American women's struggle for liberation. Presently, the social media hashtag #BlackGirlMagic, continues to proliferate across platforms such as Instagram, Twitter, and Facebook. CaShawn Thompson, a Black woman and early childhood education practitioner, inspired the hashtag when she tweeted #BlackGirlsAreMagic in 2013. Thompson's tweet was in response to a parade of online and popular media discourse that maligned and objectified Black women. The tweet sparked a national conversation, and soon after, the abbreviated phrase #BlackGirlMagic flourished as a political mandate and rallying cry to acknowledge Black women's strengths, talents, and intellectual gifts. Although the expression #BlackGirlMagic skillfully deflects attacks on African American women's personhood, the phrase largely emphasizes our victories and obscures the ideological stance that is required to cultivate the magic that we enthusiastically celebrate. On the other hand, centering the conversation on #BlackGirlJoy, shines an important light on the need for African American girls to "be in process" as they construct independent self-definitions in opposition to unrelenting structural injustices (Cooper, 2018, p. 6). Essentially, *joy* is the precursor to the *magic*.

Engendering #BlackGirlJoy, offers an approach to carving out space for African American girls to *be in process* within the context of educational institutions. Drawing on qualitative data from a two-year study of a girls' empowerment program that I established at my former high school, I argue that the Black feminist pedagogical framework that was at the core of the organization was fertile ground for cultivating #BlackGirlJoy. Moreover, through an analysis of Black feminist curricula, in-class video footage, student artifacts, and interviews with former participants, I illustrate how the specific Black feminist pedagogical framework that I employed may promote the development of more positive social and academic identities among African American girl learners in struggling schools throughout the nation.

The research presented in this book extends the work of a broad range of empirical and conceptual studies. In recent years, a litany of scholarship has focused on re-conceptualizing academic under-achievement for African American students. Regrettably, few studies in this area have focused specifically on African American girl learners, whose unique struggles are often conflated with the experiences of Black males, White girls, or girls of color. Moreover, an abundance of educational research on Black girl adolescents targets pathology through deficit-based ideologies, thereby disparaging the rich culture, intellectual prowess, and academic potential of these youth (Bartee & Brown, 2007; Fordham, 1996).

In objection to the prevalence of deficit-oriented discussions around the positioning of African American young women students, this study draws on Black feminist theory as the ideological anchor for analyzing Black girls' complex negotiations of American schooling, and the various methods by which they are (mis)educated. For centuries, Black feminist philosophy has publicly challenged the economic, political, and ideological subjugation of African American women in the United States. From Sojourner Truth's antebellum critiques of normative analyses of womanhood (Campbell, 1986), to Ransby and Matthews' (1995) contemporary examination of counter-revolutionary gender discourse in hip-hop culture, Black feminist ideology functions as "collective, oppositional knowledge" exercised by Black women as a means of self-determination and an initiative towards the collective empowerment of all oppressed people (Collins, 2000, p. 23).

In the field of education, Black feminist theory has been employed as one of many epistemological tools for investigating the recurring patterns of marginalization that threaten Black girls in P–12 schools. Much of this work purports that the growing academic underachievement of Black girl adolescents is fundamentally tied to the simultaneity of race, class, and gender oppression they endure in schools—as well as that which is present in their respective communities (Evans-Winters, 2011; Henry, 1998; Sears, 2010). Accordingly, Black feminist theory functions as a vital theoretical foundation for examining how the differential treatment of African American girl learners is rooted in a U.S. context plagued by injustice and *perpetuated* in traditional educational settings.

Recently, African American women scholars have introduced Black feminist *pedagogy* as an extension of and advancement beyond Black feminist intellectual work. Collins (2004) argues that "it is not enough to imagine empowerment for Black women in isolation from deep-seated changes in the social structure overall" (p. 3). Accordingly, the objective of Black feminist pedagogy is to subvert the social and institutional subjugation of African Americans and other subordinated groups through the use of liberating, gender-affirming classroom instruction (Mogadime, 2000; Omolade, 1993). Thus, one important aim of *Engendering #BlackGirlJoy* is to remix and re-imagine prior understandings of Black feminist pedagogy through the illumination of a framework recently applied in one large urban public school. The analyses indicate that Black feminist pedagogy, as a tool for developing viable self-identities, is an instructional practice that has the potential to serve as a buffer for African American young women. Moreover, I maintain that within the context of this study, #BlackGirlJoy emerged as a protective shield, equipping the participants with the necessary armor to combat disempowering and alienating schooling environments. Hence, the findings of this inquiry respond to the paucity of educational scholarship that examines the ways in which Black feminist teaching philosophy and curricula moves beyond the *abstraction* of critical social theory to the *implementation* of humanizing classroom practices.

Beyond the Bells: The Creation of Black Girls United

After graduating from King High School[1] in 1998, I returned five years later as a bright-eyed and enthusiastic novice English teacher. Despite subtle changes in the appearance of the school and the evolved fashion trends among students, the academic culture of King High remained the same. Disempowering pedagogies, corresponding academic disengagement, and low teacher-retention rates were the norm. Although I excelled in this environment as a student, I was well-aware of how the inequitable opportunities to learn provided inadequate priming for the social and economic mobility of most young people. With a thorough under-standing of my community's hopes and needs for education, I sought to construct a critical pedagogy (Freire, 1973; hooks, 1994) that would challenge the ways in which urban youth of color have traditionally been educated in public high schools. My initial aspirations were to utilize critical ethnic literature as a pedagogical tool to increase literacy capacities, foster empowering ethnic identities, and promote gender justice for these youth. As such, I incorporated myriad texts that explicitly resisted oppressive structures of domination through the telling of individual and collective stories—written by non-White identified individuals.

In the process of implementing this pedagogy I witnessed high levels of participation in my classes. However, in my second year of teaching, I recognized that many of my African American girl learners withdrew from class discussions involving the intersections of race, class, and gender oppression. I was astounded by how often many of these young women vehemently refrained from voicing their opinions during class conversations; yet, they did so *incredibly* via written form. This was evidenced during a unit on performance poetry, in which each student was required to develop an original poem in response to an experienced form of social or institutional oppression. Additionally, every member of the class was expected to present their writing in front their peers.

The energy of critical youth expression generated during the days leading up to student performances created an enchanting and invigorating classroom atmosphere. However, on the third afternoon of drafting, I was propelled back to reality when I learned that Ashanti, an eleventh-grade honors student, was refusing to participate in the assignment. With conviction, Ashanti informed me that she was not simply refusing to *share* her poem, she explained that she was not going to make the effort to *write* one at all! Surprised by her blatant disregard for my expectations, I utilized the best weapon in my arsenal; I called her mother, Yolanda, who later coerced Ashanti into completing the assignment. The following day, Ashanti's poem appeared on my desk, beautifully handwritten. After reading it, I immediately understood her hesitation to write and eventually perform her work in front of a group of lively and inquisitive adolescents.

In her poem, Ashanti spoke directly to her mother. Alternating between literal and figurative language, she revealed her deep reverence for and connection to Yolanda, whom she reliably consoled through multiple familial hardships. In the snippet that follows, Ashanti discusses her mother's challenges with poverty, depleting self-worth, and domestic abuse:

> Your struggle and your strife is my drive towards perfection
> Even though you're a part of me, I try to be your reflection
> Because I see a *light* in you
> And when I see your shine dimming, I try to *enlighten* you
> Even when there was no lights, no gas
> Water was cold just like life
> And there was times where I wanted to be "like Mike"
> And you was Tina cuz' pops was just like Ike
> My heart shattered at the tormenting sight
> I swear I wanted him to die every night
> The recycling fight
> The cycle of my life …

Although Ashanti eventually caved and completed the written portion of the assignment, it took a great deal of encouragement from her mother and me before she consented to reading it aloud. Her writing was deeply personal and evocative, and she did not feel safe exposing her vulnerabilities to her peers. The commotion over Ashanti's poem eventually led me to question the reason behind several other Black girl students' inconsistent participation in class discussions. I learned that there were various explanations for their resistance: many learners felt isolated by their experiences and doubted the ability of their peers to empathize; the unfamiliar practice of speaking out against racial and gender injustice made individuals uneasy; several young women were simply too frightened to vocally engage in front of other students, who they perceived to be judgmental and uninformed.

My encounter with Ashanti reified what I had already known intuitively. That is, traditional schooling environments had inculcated in these young women a general sense of powerlessness, isolation, and fear of external analytic expression. Despite my best efforts to design a curriculum that encouraged student voice and critical analysis, I came to the conclusion that I had created a classroom environment that was insufficiently empowering, relative to the needs of all of my students. Hence, I had not created a safe space for African American girl learners to *openly* engage in public critiques of their social positioning.

It is important to note that I did not come to this conclusion on my own. In numerous informal classroom encounters with Black girl adolescents, many of the young women confided in me that they occasionally felt negatively positioned by the curriculum during conversations in which we explored the intersectionalities of race and gender politics. These learners generally experienced trepidation when discussing such issues in the presence of their male-identified peers, who they believed would not understand or appreciate their unique, gendered perspectives and realities. As such, young Black women students—who were generally self-assured and outspoken—were the only individuals who openly admitted to occasionally silencing themselves in my class, to avoid feeling marginalized, attacked, and disregarded.

Because Black girls were the sole group of students who publicly expressed their discomfort in my class and displayed inconsistent patterns of classroom engagement, I felt compelled to intervene and offer an unorthodox safe space for these youth. At the time there was a special program at King High designated for young Black men as well as a separate, and somewhat popular student affinity group organized and operated by Latinx youth. Although I believed that Black boys and Latinx learners could have benefitted from additional support services at King High School, I felt it necessary to urgently intervene on behalf of Black girls who, in my opinion, were crying out for help.

Patricia Hill Collins (2000) defines a safe space as a setting in which Black women are allowed to freely engage in critical discourse around relevant issues (p. 110). Within these contexts Black women's self-defined, group standpoint emerges—which, according to Collins, is vital to U.S. Black women's survival in a shamelessly unjust society. It is through this independent, internally defined perspective that African American women generate and sustain their individual and collective activism. Traditionally, these locations have included Black churches and community organizations; although it is important to note that a distinguishing feature of a safe space is that it is free from the "surveillance of more powerful groups," such as male-identified individuals and White women (p. 111).

In an effort to combat the social and intellectual alienation my African American[2] girl learners endured, I sought to create a *safe space* for these young women to develop their critical agency—beyond the traditional classroom walls. As such, I co-founded an organization at King High entitled Black Girls United (BGU). Grounded in Black feminist theory and borrowing from the major tenets of Black feminist pedagogy, BGU functioned as an alternative and unorthodox setting within our mainstream urban schooling context. In Black Girls United, African American girl learners were afforded the opportunity to collectively read the world (Freire, 1973), and move towards transforming their place within it. Each week during lunch, members of BGU utilized critical ethnic literature to investigate and work towards resolving historical and contemporary issues that plagued U.S. African American women and girls. These student-led, Socratic seminar-based discussions often resulted in meaningful community activities that emerged organically from our conversations. In sum, the BGU members and me identified three shared objectives: to (a) engender sisterhood, (b) self-love, and (c) self-determination toward the betterment of our communities and ourselves.

Amidst a rampant culturally irrelevant schooling curriculum on campus, BGU provided a striking example of how engaging young Black women as critical thinkers helped to foster the development of empowered identities. *Engendering #BlackGirlJoy* probes deeply into *how* the organizational structure of BGU enriched participants' collective skill set to circumvent prescribed notions of Black femininity. By prioritizing the sociocultural and academic concerns and empowerment of Black girl learners, the organization was uniquely poised to catalyze individual and collective changes that I hoped would yield sustainable improvements in how Black girls at King High experienced urban schooling. To focus my research, I addressed three pressing questions that emerged from my teaching practice in Black Girls United :

1. In what ways, if any, did Black Feminist pedagogy impact the racial/ethnic and gender identities of the African American young women participating in Black Girls United?
2. In what ways, if any, did Black feminist pedagogy influence how the students in BGU *understood* their identities, as young Black women?
3. From the participants' perspectives, in what ways, if any, did BGU help students negotiate the *social* and *academic* terrains of school?

Methodology: Critical Race Feminist Autoethnography

This study utilized an autoethnographic approach to document the effects of Black feminist pedagogy on the identity development of African American girl students. Similar to other qualitative methods, autoethnography relies heavily on storytelling to assist in the interpretation of social interactions (Alexander, 1999). However, autoethnography is distinctive in that through the public exposure of personal narratives, a powerful process of self-investigation occurs. During this process, the *autobiographical* and *personal* is linked to the *cultural* and *social* (Ellis, 2004, xix). Thus, the act of self-narration fosters the critical interpretation and eventual transformation of personal, as well as broader social and political circumstances (Carey-Webb, 2001). In the case of this investigation, the narrative documentation of the effects of my teaching practice is connected to a larger socio-political project. That is, through the public, narrative disclosure of students' engagement with Black feminist pedagogy, this research aims to subvert the historically oppressive manner in which educational institutions *school* African American girl learners.

The tradition of autoethnography derives from the longstanding convention of personal storytelling in the fields of anthropology and feminist ethnography (Visweswaran, 1997). As an extension of critical race theory (Crenshaw, Gotanda, Peller, & Thomas, 1995), critical race feminism complicates the feminist practice of autobiographical storytelling within autoethnography through the centering of non-White racialized girls' experiences. As such, this autoethnography draws on critical race feminist philosophy as an effort to denaturalize Eurocentric notions of femininity within educational research practices. As young Black women authoritatively utilize their collective voice in the narrative articulation of their differential schooling experiences, the hierarchy of knowledge claims is inverted, and the "multiple layered realities in which Black girls exist" becomes the focus (Evans-Winters & Esposito, 2010, p. 22).

The voices of all 27 young Black women participants of BGU were included in my analysis of (a) field notes, (b) over 35 hours of classroom video footage during weekly lunchtime meetings, (c) student artifacts,[3] and (d) my Black feminist curriculum (weekly themes, corresponding literature, and lesson plans associated with each meeting). Additionally, I conducted two in-depth, individual interviews with a subgroup of seven participants. The selection criteria for interview participants were based on the length and patterns of student participation in the program: each of the young women selected for this study were members of BGU for its duration (fall 2005–spring 2007) who missed one or no meetings in a one-month period. Moreover, in an effort to diversify the sample, I considered variations in: (a) age, (b) positions within the school academic tracking system, (c) ethnic background, (d) degree of verbal participation in BGU, (e) relationship with the researcher, and (f) involvement in other school-related extracurricular activities.

To analyze my data sources effectively, I used Critical Discourse Analysis (Fairclough, 1995) and grounded theory (Strauss & Corbin, 1998). Thus, in my analysis of data, I looked closely at the specific structures of text as well as the sociopolitical systems and contexts in which they emerged. First, I coded the data utilizing grounded theory techniques. This included an in-depth examination of the data sources that involved identifying, labeling, categorizing, and recounting the phenomena found in the text. Thereafter, I employed selective coding in refining these categories, ultimately to contribute to developing hypotheses or building theory. In the final stages of data analysis, I searched again for supporting and disconfirming evidence for each of my initial assertions, paying closer attention to those that were substantiated across several data sources.

As a teacher–researcher, I was acutely aware of my own positionality and political interests throughout the course of this study. By virtue of the fact that I conducted research at the high school I formerly attended and at the school where I previously taught, I gained an acute awareness of the micro-politics of the research site. Although unsure of whether such conditions have skewed my data collection, I feel it is important to recognize them for the sake of revealing possible biases. Furthermore, I utilized numerous data sources and member-checking throughout to ensure that the study was presented accurately and fairly.

It is also imperative to articulate how my personal history and experiences as a Black woman have influenced the purpose of this research and the methods employed. There were multiple reasons for conducting this inquiry. One aim was to de-pathologize urban Black girls by analyzing the conditions of their racialized and gendered oppression. A second objective of this study was to unearth the pedagogical strategies that cultivated empowered social identities and intellectual gifts among the BGU participants. Finally, this research explored the means by which the aforementioned goals could be accomplished through an oppositional space of existence within the context of a school site.

Black Feminist Pedagogy as Transformative Praxis

Bearing in mind the embattled state in which Black girls find themselves, educational scholarship and theory bereft of liberatory reform efforts are "simply rhetoric contributing to cyclical patterns of marginalization and domination" (Evans-Winters, 2011, p. 11). Any educational reform strategy with the objective of democratizing schooling for young Black women must be grounded in an enhanced framework of *quality* academic instruction that belies previous efforts. Substantive, forward-thinking directives for educational policy should address two fundamental sources of sub-standard education: teacher biases, and corresponding reductive and demeaning pedagogies that undermine African American girl learners' achievement potential. By doing so, we reverse the history of denying Black women and girls access to one of the most central avenues to attaining academic success—that is, access to quality instruction.

Notwithstanding the necessity to examine the educational barriers burdening Black girl scholars, it is critical for stakeholders to become acquainted with academic contexts that engage liberatory praxis. In *Pedagogy of the Oppressed*, Paulo Freire (1973) defines praxis as "reflection and action upon the world in order to transform it" (p. 51). Through praxis, oppressed people can acquire a critical awareness of their own condition, and oppose structures of domination through the continual interplay between thought and action. Empirical scholarship by Akom (2003), Sears (2010), and Mogadime (2000) illuminate how Freire's conceptualization of praxis—enacted in unorthodox educational settings— can spark Black girls' intellectual curiosity, individual agency, and educational resilience. This research, which will be reviewed extensively in Chapter Two, contributes significantly to the field of culturally responsive pedagogy (Gay, 2000), and has implications for classroom practitioners and other professionals who are committed to eradicating the intricate web of oppression inherent in P–12 practice and curricula.

As an extension of extant scholarship, *Engendering #BlackGirlJoy* provides policymakers with data to make informed decisions when developing educational directives aimed at transforming the ways in which young Black women are positioned in schools. The implementation of new, effective reform policies is critical, as continued neglect will undoubtedly contribute to the criminalization and labor exploitation of African American girl learners, and ultimately prevent these young women from participating in society in ways that they deem meaningful. Accordingly, a critical re-examination of the conditions plaguing urban Black girl students through a Black feminist orientation can aid policymakers, scholars, and classroom practitioners in disrupting unjust schooling systems; individuals can utilize this framework to understand the various factors that contribute to these youth's academic disengagement and social and cultural disempowerment. Furthermore, engaging a Black feminist epistemological construct fosters a democratic consciousness aimed at moving society towards a "more perfect union," as articulated in our nation's Constitution.

Researching the diverse ways in which African American girl students experienced and responded to Black feminist *pedagogy* has valuable implications for classroom practice and teacher education programs. Moreover, it can likely contribute to future curriculum reform endeavors and educational research on this under-theorized and often overlooked group. Hence, this study fills a tremendous void in educational scholarship that critically addresses what young Black women want, need, and can benefit from in urban schooling contexts. The analysis uniquely centers student voices to interpret how African American girl learners are situated in schools—positioning these adolescents as experts of their socio-political location, and empowering them as co-participants in the effort to radically transform the state of U.S. public education. Lastly, it is my hope that this research contributes to the branch of educational literature illuminating the strategies employed by a substantial number of Black women teachers, like myself, as exemplars for effectively educating academically underserved youth. As Dixson and Dingus (2008) noted, the historical, navigational, and pedagogical strategies employed by Black women educators offer insights that can potentially inform the practices of *all* teachers.

Although qualitative research is often criticized for its small sample sizes and narrow applicability, the limitations of this inquiry should not overshadow its potential contribution to the field of educational research. This study utilizes narrative qualitative methods because it is particularly effective at capturing the unique, layered perspectives and experiences of the researcher and participants, thereby providing a rich contextual analysis from which grounded theory emerges and/or pre-existing theory is supported. For the seven Black girl participants, the rich counter-narratives (Solorzano & Yosso, 2002) were in many ways illustrative of the schooling experiences of numerous other African American girls in urban educational environments. The findings of this investigation will offer research-informed interventions to aid educators in developing practicable and dynamic approaches to educating this historically undervalued population of learners.

The subsequent chapters of *Engendering #BlackGirlJoy* explicate how traditional schooling contexts impact the identity development of African American girl students. I invite readers to contemplate how

Black feminist pedagogy may be used as a notable model of transformative education. Chapter Two defends the need for Black girl learners to engage in identity work explicitly, and examines relevant empirical and conceptual scholarship that highlights how urban public schooling contexts impair the development of Black girl students' race and gender identities. I conclude with an exploration of the key concepts and characteristics of Black feminist pedagogy, and the potential of this framework to foster viable social identities among African American girl adolescents. Chapter Three offers a summative breakdown of the ideological, pedagogical, and organizational structure of Black Girls United, followed by a description of the research participants and the methods I utilized. The discussion ends with an analysis of how my choice to embark on a critical race feminist autoethnography emerged out of my positionality and political interests, as someone researching at the high school I formerly attended, and the school at which I previously taught. Chapter Four draws on the concepts of *invisibility* and *hyper-visibility* to narrate the research participants' most prominent challenges to their budding identities.

After uncovering students' perceptions of how race and gender politics played out at King High School *before* they joined BGU, the book transitions into Chapters Five and Six, which illuminate the impact of my Black feminist pedagogical practice on BGU members' social identity development and schooling behaviors. Specifically, Chapter Five offers a glimpse into how the program engendered #BlackGirlJoy through the implementation of the four key elements of my Black feminist pedagogical framework (*critical feminist literature, positioning students as agents of change, a politicized ethic of care,* and *collectivity*). Chapter Six reveals the influence of Black Girls United on the race and gender identities of the participants, as well as their attachments to school. Through the inclusion of interview quotes, video transcripts from BGU classes, field notes, and student artifacts, I clarify how my Black feminist pedagogical practice engendered in students (a) an emerging critical consciousness of African American women's socio-political location, (b) an empowered sense of self that rejected popular notions of Black femininity, and (c) a more positive orientation towards school.

Finally, Chapter Seven summarizes the findings of this research and explains the implications for practitioners, teacher educators, and education reform endeavors—including specific recommendations from the participants themselves. Here, I argue that this study has the potential to aid pre-and in-service teachers in transferring critical theoretical perspectives into tangible pedagogical strategies that promote empowered social identities, increased academic engagement, and improvement in the literacies necessary for high levels of educational success.

Questions for Deeper Engagement

1. As an educator, how do you wrestle with the historical, political, and theoretical foundations of schooling in the United States?
2. How have your entangled social identities influenced your decision to teach? Discuss the ideological underpinnings that anchor you to the profession.
3. Describe the rationale for your pedagogical approach (i.e., *what*, *how*, and *why* you teach). To what degree do your methods center vulnerable student populations in your specific context?

Notes

1 This school has been given a fictitious name. Pseudonyms of institutions and participants are utilized throughout this book to protect the anonymity of the individuals involved.

2 The participants involved in BGU self-identified as Black and/or African American, although it is important to note that these young women constituted a pan-ethnic group. BGU members represented various ethnic backgrounds, including Jamaican, Belizean, and Brazilian descent, spoke a variety of languages and dialects, and held different immigration and citizenship statuses. Such varied ethnic and cultural identities contributed to the multiple perspectives among the young women, and greatly enriched the conversations and writing that took place in the organization.

3 Artifacts included tangible objects that were emblematic of a shift in identity development, such as written documents and digital media.

References

Akom, A. A. (2003). Reexamining resistance as oppositional behavior: The Nation of Islam and the creation of a Black achievement ideology. *Sociology of Education, 76,* 305–325.

Alexander, B. K. (1999). Performing culture in the classroom: An instructional (auto) ethnography. *Text and Performance Quarterly, 19,* 307–331.

Archer-Banks, D.A.M., & Behar-Horenstein, L. S. (2012). Ogbu revisited: Unpacking high-achieving African American girls' high school experiences. *Urban Education, 47*(1), 198–223.

Bartee, R. D., & Brown, C. M. (2007). *School matters: Why African American students need multiple forms of capital.* New York, NY: Peter Lang.

Beauboeuf-Lafontant, T. (2002). A womanist experience of caring: Understanding the pedagogy of exemplary Black women teachers. *The Urban Review, 34*(1), 71–86.

Bourdieu, P., & Passeron, J. (1977). *Reproduction in education, society and culture.* London, UK: Sage.

Campbell, K. H. (1986). Style and content in the rhetoric of early Afro-American feminists. *Quarterly Journal of Speech, 74*(4), 434–445.

Carey-Webb, A. (2001). *Literature and lives: A Response-based, cultural studies approach to teaching English.* Urbana, IL: National Council of Teachers of English.

Collins, P. H. (2000). *Black feminist thought: Knowledge, consciousness, and the politics of empowerment* (2nd ed.). New York, NY: Routledge.

Cooper, B. C. (2018). *Eloquent rage: A Bflack feminist discovers her superpower.* New York, NY: St. Martin's Press.

Crenshaw, K., Gotanda, N., Peller, G., & Thomas, K. (1995).*Critical race theory: The key writings that formed the movement.* New York, NY: The New Press.

Dixson, A., & Dingus, J. (2008). In search of our mother's gardens: Black women teachers and professional socialization. *Teachers College Record, 110*(4), 805–837.

Ellis, C. (2004). *The ethnographic I: A methodological novel about teaching and doing autoethnography.* Walnut Creek, CA: AltaMira.

Evans-Winters, V. E. (2011). *Teaching Black girls: Resiliency in urban classrooms* (2nd ed.). New York, NY: Peter Lang.

Evans-Winters, V. E., & Esposito, J. (2010). Other people's daughters: Critical race feminism and Black girls' education. *Educational Foundations, 24*(1/2), 11–24.

Fairclough, N. (1995). *Critical discourse analysis: The critical study of language.* New York, NY: Longman.

Fordham, S. (1996). *Blacked out: Dilemmas of race, identity, and success at Capital High.* Chicago: University of Chicago Press.

Freire, P. (1973). *Pedagogy of the oppressed.* New York, NY: Continuum Press.

Gay, G. (2000). *Culturally responsive teaching: Theory, research, and practice.* New York: Teachers College Press.

Henry, A. (1998). "Invisible" and "womanish": Black girls negotiating their lives in an African-centered school in the USA. *Race Ethnicity and Education, 1*(2), 151–170.

hooks, b. (1994). *Teaching to transgress: Education as the practice of freedom.* New York, NY: Routledge.

hooks, b. (1996). *Bone Black: Memories of girlhood.* New York, NY: Henry Holt and Company.

Love, B. (2017). A Ratchet lens: Black queer youth, agency, hip hop, and the Black ratchet imagination. *Educational Researcher, 46*(9), 539–547.

Mogadime, D. (2000). Black girls/Black women-centered texts and Black teachers as othermothers. *Journal of the Association for the Research on Mothering, 2*(2), 222–233.

Omolade, B. (1993). A Black feminist pedagogy. *Women's Studies Quarterly, 21*(1), 31–38.

Power-Carter, S. (2007). "Reading all that White crazy stuff": Black young women unpacking Whiteness in a high school British literature classroom. *Journal of Classroom Interaction, 41*(2), 42–54.

Ransby, B., & Matthews, T. (1995). Black popular culture and the transcendence of patriarchal illusions. In B. Guy-Sheftall (Ed.), *Words of fire: An anthology of African-American feminist thought* (pp. 526–535). New York, NY: The New York Press.

Sears, S. D. (2010). *The negotiation of power and identity within the Girls Empowerment Project.* Albany: SUNY Press.

Solorzano, D., & Yosso, T. (2002). Critical race methodology: Counterstorytelling as an analytical framework for education research. *Qualitative Inquiry, 8*(1), 23–44.

Strauss, A., & Corbin, J. M. (1998). *Basics of qualitative research: Techniques and procedures for developing grounded theory.* Thousand Oaks, CA: Sage.

The NAACP Legal Defense and Educational Fund & The National Women's Law Center. (2014). *Unlocking opportunity for African American girls: A call to action for educational equity.* New York, NY: Author.

Valenzuela, A. (1999). *Subtractive schooling: U.S. Mexican youth and the politics of caring.* Albany: SUNY Press.

Visweswaran, K. (1997). Histories of feminist ethnography. *Annual Review of Anthropology, 26,* 591–621.

"Feminism is not simply a struggle to end male chauvinism or a movement to ensure that women will have equal rights with men; it is a commitment to eradicating the ideology of domination that permeates Western culture on various levels- sex, race, and class to name a few- and a commitment to reorganizing society... so that the self development of people can take precedence over imperialism, expansion, and material desires."

~bell hooks

A Call for Identity Work: Black Feminist Pedagogy and Black Girl Learners

There is a pressing need for additional research in the field of education that critically examines the schooling experiences of Black girl students, as well as illuminates transformative pedagogies that engage and empower these youth. Since much of the existing literature combines the educational accounts of Black girl learners with those of their African American boy counterparts, this research overlooks how the distinctive socio-cultural positioning of Black girls influences their academic performance and schooling behaviors. In Muhammad and Dixson's (2008) large-scale quantitative analysis of high school-aged young Black women's performance in schools, the authors found that academically, African American girl learners rank in the middle among their peers and are just as likely to receive academic honors and awards. However, these students hold a lower mean test score and report less enthusiasm for their educational environments as compared to their peers. The research reveals that on most measures, Black young women acquire academic success in spite of numerous and persistent obstacles.

Historically, Black young women have encountered a unique set of challenges in U.S. schools, due in large part to the simultaneity of racist and sexist oppression in educational settings. As Muhammad and Dixson (2008) note, there is an "indivisible oneness of racialized gender experiences and feminized racial experiences" (p. 176) among African American girl students. This assertion is precisely because race is inextricably tied to gender—the schooling patterns and processes of Black students should not be examined apart from these learners' raced and gendered realities. The work of various other scholars (Evans, 1988; Grant, 1984; Morris, 2016) affirm this notion; teachers and school staff excessively and undeservedly reprimand African American girls who resist Eurocentric standards of femininity. The stereotype of the *strong Black woman*, moreover, exaggerates and romanticizes the resilience of African American girl scholars. The consequence is neglect from educational stakeholders, many of whom overlook Black girls' unique educational needs and cultural subjectivities. Disregard for the socio-political location of African American girl adolescents is exemplified in the burgeoning scholarship about the educational barriers that African American *male* students encounter. Indeed, some have argued that the emphasis on the "Black male crisis" has propelled African American girls further into the margins, and nearly renders them invisible in educational research (Crenshaw, Ocen, & Nanda, 2015; Howard, 2008; Lane, 2017).

To complicate matters, Evans-Winters and Esposito (2010) maintain that when race and gender oppression are combined with *class* inequities, Black girl learners are at an even greater disadvantage. Because these youth are more likely to live in economically depressed communities and attend poorly funded schools, they endure heightened exposure to educational resource [mal]distribution, deficit teacher ideologies, and culturally irrelevant pedagogies and curricula. The sum of these factors negatively impacts the self-concept and overall identity development of these young women, rendering their pursuit for self-actualization especially precarious and therefore difficult to sustain.

This book explores how Black feminist pedagogy—as a method of transformative education—disrupts the subordination of African American girl learners and supports the development of #BlackGirlJoy. The present chapter provides a review of the relevant literature that informs this study. I begin with a discussion of the urgent need for new educational research that critically investigates the schooling processes of African American girl adolescents. I examine empirical and conceptual scholarship highlighting the ways in which traditional urban public schooling contexts negatively influence young Black women's budding social identities, and I argue that the disempowering nature of K-12 schooling environments requires Black girls to engage in identity work to preserve their humanity. Accordingly, the subsequent section begins with an overview of the theoretical underpinnings and key concepts characteristic of Black feminist pedagogy and concludes by elucidating the implications of this teaching practice as an exemplar of identity work that fosters viable racial-ethnic identities among African American girl adolescents. Finally, this chapter culminates with a brief discussion of the limitations of the existing body of educational research that highlights the effects of Black feminist pedagogy on young Black women, as well as the significance of this study as an urgent extension of the existing scholarly literature.

The Oppressive Nature of Schooling and the Threat to Identity Development

Education as a vehicle for self-actualization and civic responsibility is one prominent feature of African American achievement ideology in general, and Black feminist praxis specifically. Historically, African American women have valued education beyond its function as a means of employability, and instead utilized formal schooling as a tool for both racial uplift and community empowerment. For instance, Maria Stewart's public intellectual discourse from the nineteenth century was a harbinger of contemporary Black feminist thought. In one of her most revered writings, Stewart encouraged Black women to utilize their intellectual talents to achieve self-definition and emerge as racial leadership figures. Stewart (1832) articulates:

> O ye daughters of Africa, awake! Awake! Arise! No longer sleep nor slumber, but distinguish yourselves. Show forth to the world that ye are endowed

with noble and exalted faculties ... I am of strong opinion that the day on which we unite heart and soul, and turn our attention to knowledge and improvement, that day the hissing and reproach among the nations of the earth against us will cease. (pp. 27–28)

Regrettably, the policies and practices in most U.S. public institutions severely limit young Black women's capacity to attain self-actualization and academic empowerment, as well as work towards community uplift. This notion is reified in Gilkes' (1983) study, where the author surveyed 25 African American women community members about their views on the purpose of formal education. These women strongly opposed the tactics applied in U.S. schools, which encouraged individuals to adopt a Eurocentric, middle-class worldview. The culture of extreme self-indulgence propagated in these spaces deterred Black women, in particular, from pursuing education as an instrument for self-improvement, community activism, and racial-ethnic empowerment.

As schools continue the tradition of promoting academic cultures that conflict with African American women's longstanding ideologies regarding education, many Black girls will actively resist these institutions. Although often criticized for its presumed essentialist stance, Black feminist theory explicitly maintains that African American women engage in varied, courageous responses to the "matrix of domination" they face (Davis, 1972, p. 82). As such, Black feminist philosophy can inform our understanding of African American girl learners' various oppositional behaviors to combat the multitude of race, class, and gender oppression that is endemic in schools.

In certain contexts, Black girls manage to remain resilient and maintain healthy racial-ethnic and gender identities in the face of marginalization and alienation. This was the case in O'Connor's (1997) case study analysis of six low-income African American high school students, two of whom were young women. The researcher revealed that individuals who had a robust, affirming sense of racial identification displayed elevated levels of self-motivation and were most committed to high academic achievement in their predominantly Black American urban high schools.

Similarly, Akom's (2003) discussion of educational resilience among Black girl adolescents echoes O'Connor's assertion that a healthy racial-ethnic group membership contributes to high academic performance among these youth. In his intensive 2-year investigation of seven successful, urban young Black women high school students, the author learned that before participants' involvement with the Nation of Islam (NOI), the young women engaged in various disruptive and often self-defeating behaviors as a means of resistance against blatant racism, teacher negligence, and the overall ineffectiveness of faculty at their school. The young women students credited their eventual social growth and educational success to their participation in the Nation of Islam, a religious entity. These learners also maintained that the cultural competency of their teachers in the NOI and the focus on strengthening the students' "racial identity, educational aspirations, and desire to uplift the black community" (p. 311) prompted their transformational attitudes and schooling behaviors.

Although students' heightened critical awareness of the racialized, gendered, and classed context in which they were schooled often resulted in politically charged conflicts with educators whom students perceived as racist or discourteous, several of the *teachers* interviewed by Akom (2003) also recognized that it was the students' activity in the Nation of Islam that led to their academic growth. The most notable gains among these youth were in their commitments to education, participation in school, leadership among their peers, and grade point averages. Thus, Akom's study disputes the theory that oppositional behaviors are threatening to the academic achievement of youth of color because they work *against* White cultural and educational norms (Ogbu, 1978; Ogbu & Simons, 1998); rather, Akom suggests that a positive racial-ethnic affiliation *assisted* these youth in confronting—and ultimately succeeding in the face of—the racist and classist culture of their school.

Additionally, Evans-Winters (2011) observed that the process of attaining educational resilience among Black girl adolescents is quite complex and often occurs under an exceptional set of circumstances. In her 2011 ethnographic study, the author examined the situational factors that aid low-income Black girls from working-class families in developing resilient behaviors. Evans-Winters defines educational resilience as "a means by which students are able to locate and identify their own strengths and the capital available to them from other people, places, and things in their immediate environment" (p. 141). The author found that for these youth, resilience was a learned process that was developed and refined over an extended period—and was, in large part, due to the aid of multiple systems of support. The bi-directional and simultaneous positive influences from family, community organizations, and school aided Black girl learners in negotiating the race, class, and gender stressors that they confronted inside and outside of educational contexts. This multi-layered support system resulted in African American girls' higher academic performance and more positive orientation towards school.

As promising as this scholarship appears, though, it is critical to note that in the studies conducted by O'Connor (1997), Akom (2003), and Evans-Winters (2011), Black girl learners heavily relied on the support of individuals and organizations *both inside* and *outside* of the school context in order to acquire and preserve their racial-ethnic, gender, and class integrity. Thus, the studies mentioned above confirm the notion that schools alone have not traditionally cultivated empowered self-identities in African American girl students. Moreover, recent educational research suggests that educational resilience and vigilance is atypical for a growing number of these learners. Analogous to the behaviors of other marginalized youth of color, countless Black girl adolescents in U.S. schools negotiate oppressive institutions by adopting actions and ideologies that are counterproductive to their academic achievement.

This trend is best evidenced by Fordham's (1993) research, which reveals how the differential treatment that Black girls experience in schools leads to varying acts of oppositional resistance. In some instances, African American girl students adopt the historically ascribed, stereotypical role of the "loud, Black girl" as a reaction against "White-defined notions of femininity" and feelings of powerlessness (Fordham, 1993, p. 13). In the context of Fordham's research, "loudness" often has an adverse effect on the academic achievement of Black girl learners—such demeanor is traditionally characterized as subversive and threatening to Eurocentric prescriptions of gender that are typically reinforced in schools. The scholarship of Lei (2003) and Morris (2007) further indicate that African American girl adolescents' teachers and peers disproportionately perceive these youth as unladylike in comparison to their White, Asian, and Latina counterparts. As such, education stakeholders frequently regard Black girls as openly defiant, loud, and aggressive— behaviors aligned with stereotypical notions of Black femininity—and often target these learners as the source of their frustrations.

Grant (1984) confirms that the recurrent "race-gender differentiated socialization" of Black girls—combined with educators' misunderstanding of these students' dispositions and sensibilities—makes these youth especially vulnerable to harsh punishment in schools (p. 98). Additionally, Grant notes that numerous African American girl adolescents' adoption of adverse social roles and behaviors stems from a deep desire to be acknowledged, valued, and respected by their teachers and peers. Consequently, educators often misinterpret these learners' self-reliance and assertiveness as defiance, as opposed to precociousness.

Subsequent works by Winn (2010a, 2010b), Blake, Butler, Lewis, and Darensbourg (2011), and Crenshaw et al. (2015) extend Grant's findings. Collectively, these studies indicate that *urban* Black girl learners most frequently negotiate excessive reprimand in schools. The over-representation of African American young women in exclusionary disciplinary practices and discipline sanctions—referrals, in-school and out-of-school suspensions, expulsions, and more—poses a grave danger to this population of learners. Winn (2010a, 2010b) contends that the social isolation that young Black women experience significantly threatens their self-esteem and perceptions of self-worth, and increases the likelihood that these adolescents will have a future in the juvenile and criminal justice systems. Thus, in urban settings, the mechanisms by which schooling environments shape identity are far more complicated for African American girls. These youth are not only burdened by ubiquitous pressures to conform to socio-cultural standards of White femininity, but they must also learn to navigate academically disenfranchised and under-resourced schooling environments that are fixated on Black girls' surveillance, containment, and punishment.

For many high-achieving Black girl adolescents, the pressure to conform to Eurocentric gender norms similarly results in self-defeating behaviors. However, instead of internalizing the stereotype of the "loud black girl," these youth engage in what Fordham (1996) calls *ethnic disassociation*. Fordham argues that some high-achieving Black girls purposefully use silence and invisibility to maintain a non-threatening, raceless persona. In other words, these young women strategically utilized ethnic disassociation as an attempt to avoid the extreme judgment and alienation experienced by others who embrace an ascribed Black identity. Although this strategy often results in high academic achievement, it has a negative impact on these young women, whose self-alienation encourages both "psychological and physical separation from the broader African American community" (Robinson & Ward, 1991, p. 93).

Furthermore, Stephanie Carter's (2007) research is consistent with Fordham's findings and calls attention to how African American girl learners are regularly negotiating Whiteness within required high school curricula. In addition to socio-linguistic and ethnographic methods, Carter utilizes a Black feminist epistemological frame to explore the impact of traditional curriculum on the budding and fragile identities of Black girl learners. Carter's critical analysis of the educational experiences of young Black women high school students reveals the academic and psychological struggles that these youth endure as their identities are incessantly challenged throughout schooling. For instance, the research suggests that many Black girl adolescents have a particular view of the contradictions between the actions and ideologies of the dominant group, as compared to their own experiences and beliefs (Collins, 2000). Because young Black women use their racial and gendered identities as paradigmatic frames to understand what happens in their classrooms, many of these learners are compelled to disassociate from their race-gender identities and conform to Eurocentric socio-cultural norms to avoid alienation and increase their prospects for favorable educational outcomes.

In sum, the empirical literature centering the K-12 schooling experiences of Black girl students exposes the extensive history of oppression and alienation these young women experience in educational institutions and their prolonged use of various protective mechanisms as means of survival and self-preservation. Whether resisting via racial disassociation, internalizing reductive images of Black womanhood, or deliberately embodying a positive racial-ethnic identity, Black girls respond to degrading schooling environments in varied and unrelenting ways. Hence, this scholarship glaringly demonstrates the pressing need for the Black girl scholar to *explicitly* engage in *identity work* (a) to preserve her integrity, (b) increase her potential of achieving academic success, and (c) ultimately expand the possibilities of her socio-political future.

The Necessity for Black Girls to Engage in Identity Work

In her article "(Un)necessary Toughness?: Those 'Loud Black Girls' and Those 'Quiet Asian Boys,'" Joy Lei (2003) suggests that identity construction is "an active and dynamic process through which an individual identifies himself or herself in relation to how he or she is constituted as a subject by dominant discourses and representations" (p. 159). Thus, in the case of the Black girl learner, one's self-concept is gradually developed over time, *in response to* and *as a product of* dominant narratives around the meaning of African American femininity. Considering the historical, unabated denigration of Black women in larger society and the corresponding stereotypical depictions of African American women and girls in popular media, one can infer that young Black women must incessantly negotiate "fixed categorizations" and "monolithic depictions" of what it means to be both Black *and* a girl adolescent in the United States (p. 159). Additionally, and as mentioned previously, schools reproduce prevalent images of young Black girls as aggressive and anti-intellectual through the curriculum, peer interactions, and culturally irresponsible pedagogical practices, which perpetuate the cultural hegemony that is rampant in our society.

It is critical to address the interplay between schooling processes and one's racial-ethnic identity, as researchers have discovered a strong correlation between the two. Although some scholars have argued that significant racial-ethnic ties result in greater vulnerability to negative stereotypes (Ogbu, 2003; Steele, 1997), others have purported that adolescents who have developed a secure, positive attachment to their ethnicity *and* can critically analyze the societal messages they encounter are far less likely to internalize the controlling images regarding their racial-ethnic group (Townsend et al., 2010; Ward, 1990). Furthermore, a plethora of research intimates that individuals demonstrating a strong attachment and sense of pride regarding racial-ethnic group membership are more likely to hold a positive self-perception of their academic abilities and more optimistic feelings about school overall (Cokley & Chapman, 2008; Wright, 2011).

For these reasons, some education scholars have argued in favor of protective mechanisms *within* schools that support Black girl students in developing empowering racial/ethnic identities. As public K-12 institutions willfully continue the tradition of denying African American girls opportunities to cultivate viable racial-ethnic and gender identities, these young women must overtly and strategically engage in *identity work* as a buffer against harmful race, gender, and class stereotypes. According to Collins (2000), *identity work* is a process by which Black women acknowledge, analyze, and engage in resistance against structures of oppression. Black women's collective endeavor to self-actualize has historically taken place in women's clubs and churches—apart from conventional school sites. However, as Henry (2009) notes, the necessity for *identity work* among African American girls within schools is ever-pressing. Working towards self-definition and self-reliance in educational spaces has the potential to challenge the estrangement these youth experience by disrupting the social scripts and dominant race-gender schema that devalue Black femininity. Moreover, alternative settings support young Black women in nurturing their individual and collective voices and create an opportunity to engage in constructive acts of oppositional resistance, which may result in more promising academic and life trajectories.

U.S. Black Feminist Philosophy and Pedagogy

The research presented in *Engendering #BlackGirlJoy* explores Black feminist pedagogy as a means of *identity work* for African American girl learners in one urban high school. Educational researchers have utilized a plethora of theoretical approaches to understand the academic experiences, struggles, and achievement of Black girls. Among those explored, Black feminist *theory* remains one of the most comprehensive socio-historical lenses and voices of authority for framing the schooling experiences of Black girls in light of the intersecting oppressions they face. As a critical social theory, Black feminism posits that African American women have historically faced interlocking forms of systemic oppression, which include economic, political, and ideological stratification. From labor and sexual exploitation, to denial of the rights and privileges extended to White male citizens, and the reductive and demeaning stereotypes of mammies, jezebels, welfare queens, and emasculating sapphires—Black feminist philosophy contends that African American women in the United States have been violently positioned as the "objectified other" (Collins, 2000, p. 70). The differential treatment these women endure transcends class, age, geography, and sexual orientation, and ultimately gives rise to Black women's distinctive consciousness. This collective consciousness, or "self-defined standpoint" (Lorde, 1984; Shaw, 1991), is a perilous threat to African American women's prescribed subordination.

Furthermore, Black feminism challenges the notion that African American political activism belongs exclusively to men, as well as the belief that feminist ideology and practice belongs solely to White women (Hull, Bell-Scott, & Smith, 1982). Cashmore (1996) describes a Black feminist stance as "rethinking Black experiences from a feminist perspective and revising White feminist politics from an Afrocentric perspective" (p. 20). Functioning as shared, oppositional knowledge birthed at the margins of society, Black feminist praxis operates in the interest of freedom for all oppressed people—however, it centralizes Black women's subjugation and activism by placing them at the locus of analysis. Thus, to eradicate all group oppression, it is critical to struggle for the recognition of African American women's inherent humanity and profound intellectual faculties.

Because schools are microcosms of communities, Black feminist theorists argue that the ways in which young African American women experience racism, sexism, and classism in their neighborhoods is often mirrored in their experiences at school. As formerly discussed, societal disassociation with young Black women is revealed in schools when youth are systematically disengaged through de-humanizing pedagogies and disproportionately channeled into educational pathways that lead to criminalization. Regrettably, the othering of this population of learners is later reproduced in these women's subjugated labor positions and resulting racial and spatial isolation to urban ghettos (Anyon, 2005; Ladson-Billings, 2000). As such, situating African American girls' institutional oppressions within a Black feminist framework is valuable because its anti-deficit, anti-pathological stance subverts dominant racist ideologies about Black girls by highlighting how these women endure various instances of marginality at the crossroads of their multiple identities.

Finally, it is imperative to note that fundamental to Black feminism is the acknowledgment that Black feminist *philosophy* is generated to inspire collective *action*. Hence, a Black feminist perspective on contemporary schooling inequities (a) magnifies the visibility of systematic educational injustices imposed on African American girl adolescents, (b) highlights their varied forms of oppositional behavior, and (c) offers urgent and useful methods toward creating liberatory learning environments for these young women. As African American women have historically engaged in theoretical examinations of the interlocking forms of oppression they endure, they have simultaneously utilized their oppositional knowledge as a means to resist prescribed subordination. Within the field of education, Black feminist *pedagogy* is the product of a merger between theory and activism. Despite its relatively recent appearance in educational scholarship (Joseph, 1995; Omolade, 1993), Black feminist pedagogy has an extensive history among African American women educators, most of whom explicitly situate their practice within a Black feminist/womanist politic (Higginbotham, 1995; Ladson-Billings & Henry, 1990; Washington, 1987). Inspired by the philosophy "lifting as we climb," these Black woman teachers employed a variety of pedagogies reflecting their appreciation for education as a tool for social mobility as well as a means of personal and community empowerment.

Rooted in a history of oppression and activism, Black feminist pedagogical practice is birthed out of the belief that without an explicitly transformative pedagogy, Black women and girls will continue to be overlooked as contributors to U.S. intellectual production and will be unseen as beneficial to the learning environment. As such, Black feminist pedagogy is situated under the umbrella of critical pedagogy (Freire, 1973; Giroux & McLaren, 1994) and applied with the clear intention of subverting structural inequities by equipping students with the necessary tools to critically analyze and eventually *thrive through* the various social and institutional barriers they face.

Notwithstanding the initial function of Black feminist pedagogy to empower African American students collectively, some educational researchers have taken particular interest in analyzing how these practices influence *Black girls'* academic engagement and self-determination. Scholars such as Henry (2009) and Sears (2010) propose that Black feminist pedagogy may be particularly useful in the instruction of these young women, who are consequently experiencing increased rates of academic disengagement, declining test scores, and devolving self-worth as a result of the reductive and disesteeming curricula and pedagogies in schools. Currently, an abundance of researchers have conceptualized, re-conceptualized, and extended the features of Black feminist pedagogy, thereby creating a dynamic and nuanced framework. To study the utility of this practice as a method for instructing Black girl learners, we must first delineate the defining features that set it apart from other anti-oppressive pedagogical strategies.

Education as Liberation

Black feminist educators understand that the practice of teaching for liberation is in direct conflict with the historic role of the institution as a source of oppression. hooks (1994) contends that under these circumstances, it is particularly crucial for Black feminist educators to maintain an acute awareness of their positionality and openly engage in practices that are steadily "at odds with the existing [oppressive] structure" (p. 135). The political clarity among Black womanist educators is grounded in the belief that they are both "ethically and ethnically" accountable for preparing African American youth to transcend socio-political injustices—such a philosophy is heavily reflected in their curricular choices (Beauboeuf-Lafontant, 2002, p. 77).

Higginbotham (1995) defines Black feminist pedagogy as an instructional technique that centralizes conversations about how schools systematically teach Eurocentric "misinformation" through curricula and informally communicate these ideologies through social interactions (p. 485). As such, Black feminist classrooms function as analytic spaces where students confront dominant discourses that subjugate raced, classed, and gendered collectivities. This method of "truth-telling," according to Joseph (1995), presents both students and teachers with alternative ways of constructing and validating knowledge about their realities. In this way, Black feminist pedagogy counters the exclusivity of traditional Eurocentric curricula, which highlights the achievements and perspectives of White men and omits and distorts the realities of people of color—and women of color, in particular (Joseph, 1995, p. 466).

On the other hand, teaching that is reflective of Black feminist philosophy utilizes the classroom as a site of resistance, in which practitioners give students varied opportunities to engage in what hooks (1989, 1994) describes as "coming to voice." The author maintains that students are empowered through collective participation when educators create space in the curriculum for all individuals to engage in dialogue, as well as through the instructor's recognition of the distinctiveness of each student's point of view. The unambiguous acknowledgment within Black feminist pedagogy of how individuals uniquely contribute to the production of knowledge is humanizing for both students *and* teachers, reflecting the liberatory nature of education as a practice of freedom. This philosophy of schooling as a political endeavor is also mirrored in Black feminist educators' response to the holistic needs of their students through *othermothering*.

Othermothering

The tradition of othermothering in African American communities has an extensive history as a practice of freedom, dating back to the earliest days of slavery in the United States. Defined by Collins (2000) as "women who assist blood-mothers by sharing mothering responsibilities" (p. 178), othermothers in the larger social context customarily cater to the needs of neighborhood children as a means of assisting biological parents who *may* or *may not* lack the resources or the ability to properly care for them. Foster (1993) documents how the inherited tradition of shared responsibility is apparent in the teaching philosophies and pedagogies of contemporary Black feminist educators. The role of these women extends beyond academic support and includes nurturing kinlike relationships—wherein teachers attend to students' social, emotional, and psychological development.

Beauboeuf-Lafontant (2002) characterizes Black feminist educators' "embrace of the maternal" as one measure of their genuine commitment to the success of every student (p. 72). Commonly exhibited by home visits, frequent collaboration with parents and overall student advocacy, Black women's othermothering is both relational and political. For instance, in a study conducted by Case (1997), the biographical portraits of two urban elementary school educators revealed the embedded nature of the practitioners' "collective social conscience" in their everyday actions and overall philosophy of education as a means for racial uplift (p. 36). In essence, the work of Black feminist othermothers on behalf of the African American community is one of many examples of these women's expression of personal accountability. Moreover, othermothering is also a cultural strategy reflective of Black women's *politicized ethic of care.*

A Politicized Ethic of Care

Roseboro and Ross (2009) draw on a womanist pedagogy to examine the role of colorblindness and care theory as related to liberatory, anti-Eurocentric practice. The authors posit that Black women's "liberatory ethic of care" is grounded in their unique ideologies and practices around (a) work and care, (b) freedom and choice, and (c) authority and power (p. 34). Accordingly, Black womanist educators strategically perform caring in classrooms by providing students with the necessary tools to navigate social and political barriers to freedom. In this context, caring is "infused with love, humility, passion, and power" and demonstrated by unrelenting displays of personal accountability and collective responsibility (p. 36). Thus, the historicized understanding among Black feminist educators to view care as inherent to their practice gives rise to a concurrently political *and* emotional framework for the instruction of African American learners.

hooks (2003) discounts the dehumanizing yet conventional system of extracting emotion from the practice of teaching. One drawback of pedagogies devoid of an emotional connection—namely *love*—is that such methods prevent teachers from gauging and attending to the emotional climate of their students, which could potentially interfere with each student's ability and desire to learn. Hence, hooks contends that teaching with love affords educators the clarity to appropriately tailor the mood of a classroom and set the foundation for building community among students and the instructor. Essentially, a deeply rooted emotional investment in one's practice is central to Black feminist teaching philosophy and has historical significance as a critical component of Black feminist pedagogy.

Education as liberation, *othermothering*, and a *politicized ethic of care* function interdependently as three core elements of Black feminist pedagogy. While these three conceptual strands are woven into the fabric of Black feminist pedagogical literature, they have not *all* been explicitly mentioned or jointly utilized in research contexts in which Black girls were the foci. The next section explores the distinctive means by which scholars apply Black feminist pedagogy to conduct empirical research that centers Black girl adolescents.

Paving the Path: Black Feminist Pedagogy and Research with Black Girls

A few important studies have highlighted the effects of Black feminist pedagogy on Black girl learners' identity development and participation in school. Henry's (1998) research is a harbinger of this work. Her study unveiled the ways in which African American elementary school girls frequently positioned themselves as passive and voiceless in coeducational settings, yet appeared outspoken and intellectually self-assured outside of the classroom. In an effort to combat the patriarchal and racial subordination Black girls frequently endure in school, Henry (2009) conducted a separate study in which she designed an unorthodox space for middle school-aged Afro Caribbean girls to engage in the Black feminist pedagogical practice that hooks (1989) coined as *coming to voice*. Through "reflexive literacy research methods," Henry crafted a reading and writing project that fostered the development of critical literacies among these youth (p. 164). One of the intriguing findings of Henry's work is that when young African American women were challenged to unlearn the ascribed, gendered behaviors of passivity and conformity, these individuals were intellectually empowered by their ability to problem-pose and problem-solve effectively around issues relevant to their unique identities.

Mogadime's (2000) study similarly illuminated the effects of Black feminist pedagogical practices employed in unconventional educational contexts within schools. Her research documented the experience of one "community othermother" who embraced the task of developing a separate lunchtime and afterschool drama program for Black girls as a "site of resistance" against the largely Eurocentric school curriculum (p. 223). In direct contrast to standard pedagogies, the Black girl-centered curriculum described in Mogadime's study included numerous counternarratives, which functioned as a "pedagogy of hope" and were emblematic of the transformative potential of each student's life (p. 229). Although this study was conducted in Southern Ontario, Canada, we can extrapolate from the outcomes of Mogadime's research and gain insight into the potential of Black feminist pedagogies and curricula as a strategy towards democratizing education for urban young Black women in the United States.

For instance, Sears's (2010) scholarship is an extension of Mogadime's findings. Her ethnographic research documented the usefulness of womanist pedagogies in a community-based all-girls organization, suitably named the Girls Empowerment Project (GEP). Initiated to address the race, gender, and class oppression these youth experienced in schools and in their respective communities, the GEP functioned as a safe space for young Black women to critique the ways in which their identities were both reflective of and in opposition to dominant discourses that malign urban Black girls. According to Sears, "Africentric womanist" ideology and pedagogy separated students from their ascribed subordinated identities; provided them with tools to negotiate power relationships; and fostered ethnic pride, intellectual engagement, and community solidarity (p. 117).

By documenting the social and academic outcomes of Black feminist pedagogies in relation to African American girl students, the scholarship of Henry (1998, 2009), Mogadime (2000), and Sears (2010) has tremendous implications for teaching, learning, and research in urban schooling contexts. The carefully crafted "safe spaces" discussed in the literature functioned as "sites of resistance" where the implementation of Black feminist/womanist curricula and corresponding pedagogies catered to the cultural subjectivities of Black girl students as a multiply oppressed group. These studies provide pedagogical models for practitioners to utilize to engage African American girls in healthy oppositional behaviors—such as the pursuit of excellence as a site of resistance—which directly conflicts with social and institutional forces that socialize young Black women to be silent, accommodating, and passive recipients of schooling.

Notwithstanding the significant contributions of Black feminist pedagogical research to educational literature, hooks (1994) reminds us that engaged pedagogies must acknowledge the uniqueness of *every* classroom. She suggests that instructional methods must "constantly be changed, invented, [and] re-conceptualized to address each new teaching experience" (p. 10). As such, it is critical to note that proponents of Black feminist pedagogy do not imply or project one defined set of practices to address the varied academic, emotional, and socio-cultural needs of young Black women. Rather, it does offer constructive strategies for educators to cultivate African American girl learners' critical social consciousness, intellectual curiosity, and collective agency to improve their academic and social lives.

What is still missing from extant research, though, is a rich, empirical analysis of how a *holistic* application of Black feminist pedagogy impacts the social identities and educational experiences of African American girl adolescents over an *extended* period of time, *within* U.S. urban public schools. Building on the work of previous scholarship, the data presented in *Engendering #BlackGirlJoy* represents my work of closely following African American girl learners throughout two academic school years. In particular, I have relied on the rich and descriptive narratives of these individuals to examine how Black feminist pedagogy influenced the development of their racial/ethnic and gender identities and orientation towards school. The accounts of these students offer new insights into conceptualizing and applying Black feminist praxis in an urban context, illuminating new theories and areas of significance that have yet to be explored in educational research. Additionally, various tenets of Black feminist pedagogy were applied *simultaneously*, as opposed to highlighting one or two defining features—the trend in previous studies. I argue that the holistic application of these unique tenets (a) had an added effect at uprooting the hegemony embedded in standard classroom settings and (b) ultimately engaged the African American girl participants' academic potential, intellectual agency, and self-actualization.

Questions for Deeper Engagement

1. This chapter centers Black feminist theory as the theoretical lens. Discuss alternative conceptual frameworks that might enhance our understanding of African American girl adolescents' schooling experiences and their relationship to structure and power.
2. The rapid demographic changes that the twentieth century birthed has complicated the longstanding belief that public schools should uphold American culture. Teachers regularly view working-class learners, immigrants, and Students of Color as culturally inferior. Drawing on an educational theory that resonates with you, discuss how your curricular practices disrupt the estrangement

of non-dominant student populations—and highlight potential areas of growth in your practice.

References

Akom, A. A. (2003). Reexamining resistance as oppositional behavior: The Nation of Islam and the creation of a Black achievement ideology. *Sociology of Education, 76*(4), 305–325.

Anyon, J. (2005). *Radical possibilities: Public policy, urban education, and a new social movement.* New York, NY: Routledge.

Beauboeuf-Lafontant, T. (2002). A womanist experience of caring: Understanding the pedagogy of exemplary Black women teachers. *The Urban Review, 34*(1), 71–86.

Blake, J., Butler, B., Lewis, C., & Darensbourg, A. (2011). Unmasking the inequitable discipline experienced of urban Black girls: Implications for urban educational stakeholders. *The Urban Review, 43*(1), 90–106.

Carter, S. P. (2007). "Reading all that White crazy stuff ": Black young women unpacking Whiteness in a high school British literature classroom. *Journal of Classroom Interaction, 41*(2), 42–54.

Case, K. I. (1997). African American othermothering in the urban elementary school. *The Urban Review, 29*(1), 25–39.

Cashmore, E. (1996). *Dictionary of race and ethnic relations* (4th ed.). New York, NY: Routledge.

Cokley, K., & Chapman, C. (2008). The roles of ethnic identity, anti-white attitudes and academic self- concept in African American student achievement. *Social Psychology of Education, 11*(4), 349–365.

Collins, P. H. (2000). *Black feminist thought: Knowledge, consciousness, and the politics of empowerment* (2nd ed.). New York, NY: Routledge.

Crenshaw, K. W., Ocen, P., & Nanda, J. (2015). *Black girls matter: Pushed out, overpoliced, and underprotected.* New York, NY: African American Policy Forum and the Center for Intersectionality and Social Policy Studies. Retrieved from http://static1.square-space.com/static/53f20d90e4b0b80451158d8c/t/54dcc1ece4b001c03e323448/1423753708557/AAPF_BlackGirlsMatterReport.pdf

Davis, A. (1972). Reflections on the Black woman's role in the community of slaves. *The Massachusetts Review, 13*(1/2), 81–100.

Evans, G. (1988). Those loud black girls. In D. Spender & E. Sarah (Eds.), *Learning to lose: Sexism and education* (Vol. 2, pp. 183–190). London, UK: Women's Press.

Evans-Winters, V. E. (2011). *Teaching Black girls: Resiliency in urban classrooms* (2nd ed.). New York, NY: Peter Lang.

Evans-Winters, V. E., & Esposito, J. (2010). Other people's daughters: Critical race feminism and Black girls' education. *Educational Foundations, 24*(1/2), 11–24.

Fordham, S. (1993). "Those loud Black girls": (Black) women, silence, and gender "passing" in the academy. *Anthropology and Education Quarterly, 24*(1), 3–32.

Fordham, S. (1996). *Blacked out: Dilemmas of race, identity, and success at Capital High.* Chicago: University of Chicago Press.

Foster, M. (1993). Othermothers: Exploring the educational philosophy of Black American women teachers. In M. Arnot & K. Weiler (Eds.), *Feminism and social justice in education: International perspectives* (pp. 101–123). Washington, D.C.: Falmer Press.

Freire, P. (1973). *Pedagogy of the oppressed.* New York, NY: Continuum Press.

Gilkes, C. T. (1983). Going up for the oppressed: The career mobility of Black women community workers *Journal of Social Issues, 39*(3), 115–139.

Giroux, H., & McLaren, P. (1994). *Between borders: Pedagogy and the politics of cultural studies.* New York, NY: Routledge.

Grant, L. (1984). Black females' "place" in desegregated classrooms. *Sociology of Education, 57*(2), 98–111.

Henry, A. (1998). "Invisible" and "womanish": Black girls negotiating their lives in an African-centered school in the USA. *Race Ethnicity and Education, 1*(2), 151–170.

Henry, A. (2009). "Speaking up" and "speaking out": Examining "voice" in a reading/writing program with adolescent African Caribbean girls. *Journal of Literacy Research, 30*(2), 233–252.

Higginbotham, E. (1995). Designing an inclusive curriculum: Bringing all women into the core. In B. Guy-Sheftall (Ed.), *Words of fire: An anthology of African-American feminist thought* (pp. 473–476). New York, NY: The New York Press.

hooks, b. (1989). *Talking back: Thinking feminist, thinking Black.* Boston, MA: South End Press.

hooks, b. (1994). *Teaching to transgress: Education as the practice of freedom.* New York, NY: Routledge.

hooks, b. (2003). *Teaching community: A pedagogy of hope.* New York, NY: Routledge.

Howard, T. C. (2008). "Who really cares?" The disenfranchisement of African American males in preK-12 schools: A critical race theory perspective. *Teachers College Record, 110*(5), 954–985.

Hull, G. T., Bell-Scott, P., & Smith, B. (1982). *All the women are white, and all the Blacks are men, but some of us are brave: Black women's studies.* Old Westbury, NY: Feminist Press.

Joseph, G. I. (1995). Black feminist pedagogy and schooling in White capitalist America. In B. Guy-Sheftall (Ed.), *Words of fire: An anthology of African-American feminist thought* (pp. 462–471). New York, NY: The New York Press.

Ladson-Billings, G. (2000). Fighting for our lives: Preparing teachers to teach African American students. *Journal of Teacher Education, 51*(3), 206–214.

Ladson-Billings, G., & Henry, A. (1990). Blurring the borders: Voices of African liberatory pedagogy in the United States and Canada. *Journal of Education, 172*(2), 72–88.

Lane, M. (2017). Reclaiming our queendom: Black feminist pedagogy and the identity formation of African American girls. *Equity & Excellence in Education, 50*(1), 13–24.

Lei, J. L. (2003). (Un)necessary toughness? Those "loud Black girls" and those "Quiet Asian boys." *Anthropology and Education Quarterly, 34*(2), 158–181.

Lorde, A. (1984). *Sister outsider: Essays and speeches.* Berkeley, CA: Crossing Press.

Mogadime, D. (2000). Black girls/Black women-centered texts and Black teachers as othermothers. *Journal of the Association for the Research on Mothering, 2*(2), 222–233.

Morris, E. W. (2007). "Ladies" or "loudies"? Perceptions and experiences of Black girls in classrooms. *Youth and Society, 38*(4), 490–515.

Morris, M. (2016). *Pushout: The criminalization of Black Girls in Schools.* New York, NY: The New Press.

Muhammad, C. G., & Dixson, A. D. (2008). Black females in high school: A statistical educational profile. *The Negro Educational Review, 59*(3–4), 163–180.

O'Connor, C. (1997). Dispositions toward (collective) struggle and educational resilience in the inner city: A case analysis of six African American high school students. *American Educational Research Journal, 34*(4), 593–629.

Ogbu, J. (2003). *Black American students in an affluent suburb: A study of academic disengagement.* Mahwah, NJ: Erlbaum.

Ogbu, J., & Simons, H. D. (1998). Voluntary and involuntary minorities: A cultural-ecological theory of school performance with some implications for education. *Anthropology and Education Quarterly, 29,* 155–188.

Omolade, B. (1993). A Black feminist pedagogy. *Women's Studies Quarterly, 21*(1), 31–38.

Robinson, T., & Ward, N. L. (1991). *Women, girls & psychotherapy: Reframing resistance.* Binghamton, NY: The Haworth Press.

Roseboro, D. L., & Ross, S. N. (2009). Care-sickness: Black women educators, care theory, and a hermeneutic of suspicion. *Educational Foundations, 23*(3/4), 19–40.

Sears, S. D. (2010). *The negotiation of power and identity within the Girls Empowerment Project.* Albany: SUNY Press.

Shaw, S. J. (1991). Black club women and the creation of the National Association of Colored Women. *Journal of Women's History, 3*(2), 11–25.

Steele, C. (1997). A threat in the air: How stereotypes shape intellectual identity and performance. *American Psychologist, 52*(6), 613–629.

Stewart, M. (1832). Productions of Mrs. Maria W. Stewart. In B. Guy-Sheftall (Ed.), *Words of fire: An anthology of Black feminist thought* (pp. 26–29). New York, NY: The New Press.

Townsend, T. G., Neilands, T. B., Jones-Thomas, A., & Jackson, T. R. (2010). I'm no jezebel; I am young, gifted, and Black: Identity, sexuality, and Black girls. *Psychology of Women Quarterly, 34*(3), 273–285.

Ward, J. V. (1990). Racial identity formation and transformation. In C. Gilligan, N. D. Lyons, & T. J. Hanmer (Eds.), *Making connections: The relational worlds and adolescent girls at Emma Willard School* (pp. 215–238). Cambridge: Harvard University Press.

Washington, M. H. (1987). How racial differences helped us discover our common ground. In M. Culley & C. Portuges (Eds.), *Gendered subjects: The dynamics of feminist teaching* (pp. 221–229). Boston, MA: Routledge & Kegan Paul.

Winn, M. T. (2010a). "Betwixt and between": Literacy, liminality, and the celling of Black girls. *Race Ethnicity and Education, 12*(4), 425–447.

Winn, M. T. (2010b). "Our side of the story": Moving incarcerated youth voices from margins to center. *Race, Ethnicity and Education, 13*(3), 313–325.

Wright, B. L. (2011). I know who I am, do you? Identity and academic achievement of successful African American male adolescents in an urban pilot high school in the United States. *Urban Education, 46*(4), 611–638.

"Research is formalized curiosity. It is poking and prying with a purpose."

~ *Zora Neale Hurston*

Chapter Three

Organized Turmoil: A Struggling School with Boundless Potential

We had kids from all sorts of backgrounds. Somebody whose family is from Honduras on my left, and then, like a Black girl from Jamaica would be on my right! And we were lucky because we actually had teachers from a lot of different backgrounds, too. And I really believe that most of my teachers were *really* smart. And the principal and administrators and stuff, too. But, for some reason—I don't know why—they just could *not* get it together! (Erykah, former Black Girls United member)

Located in Los Angeles' historic Slauson District, King High School[1] was a largely residential urban community. By 2005, the area, which was once entirely African American, had evolved into a sprawling multi-ethnic locale. The student population at King High, which consisted of roughly 2,000 youth in 2005, represented the diversity of the neighborhood. Although typically grouped into broad categories such as Black (66 percent) and Hispanic (33 percent), the individuals in this learning community represented a wide range of ethnic backgrounds that directly influenced the social and academic climate of the school. King High was a microcosm of its surrounding community of residents with strong African American, Belizean, Jamaican, Mexican, Guatemalan, and Salvadoran roots. This unique blend of ethnicity, family histories, and language created a pressing need for an educational atmosphere that catered to the specific subjectivities of this culturally enriched student body.

In addition to serving an ethnically and racially distinct population, King High School was home to an overwhelming number of youth whose family incomes ranged from below the poverty line to low-income. In 2005, approximately half of the student body was labeled "socioeconomically disadvantaged" by the California Department of Education. The exceptionally high number of materially under-resourced learners qualified King High School for Title 1 assistance—a federally funded, compensatory education program that supplemented the core curriculum and regular school services. The purpose of the organization was to shepherd a range of resources and supports through the school to mitigate the impact of adverse community conditions on students' educational outcomes. Accordingly, under Title 1, students, parents, and staff received tutoring services, access to an on-site school psychologist, parenting classes, and staff development. Supplementary program components that were provided through Title 1 also included literacy intervention programs, field trips, assemblies, and assisted infusion of technology into the standard curriculum. Among the primary objectives of the federal aid was to offer King High School students equitable opportunities to obtain a high-quality education—and reach, at a minimum, proficiency on state academic achievement standards and assessments. A fragmented examination of King High School would indicate that the ancillary funding might improve stakeholders' efforts to foster a rigorous and vibrant educational environment. However, as Erykah noted in the opening excerpt, King High had gained notoriety as a struggling school, fraught with untapped potential.

The devastating dynamics of racism and a post-industrial landscape of poverty sidled into the classrooms at King High, where wounds and dreams intermingled. During the 2004–2005 academic year, the school's base Academic Performance Index (API) of 505 earned a statewide rank of 1—the lowest percentile among other majority Black schools within the State of California. After six years of failing to meet the adequate yearly progress (AYP) criteria required by the No Child Left Behind mandates, King High's administration received an alarming wake-up call before the start of the 2005–2006 academic term. A letter from the Western Association of Schools and Colleges (WASC) informed school stakeholders of their loss of accreditation. Two evaluations from visits by accrediting teams within a two-year period constituted the judgment. During the assessments, the WASC team identified low academic standards, the lack of a school-wide action plan, behavioral defiance, poor student attendance, and rampant student tardiness. To the dismay of school personnel, students, parents, and the larger Slauson District community, King High had earned the disreputable title of the first school in the district to lose its WASC accreditation.

Despite several years of extreme academic failure and the recent loss of accreditation, the faculty and staff at King High exhibited impenetrable resilience. Educators' principal concern was to bridge students who lag behind to levels of academic proficiency. Regrettably, the revolving door of school leadership and the questionable directives[2] of the district restricted their efforts. Consequently, rampant student disengagement, high student and faculty transiency, increasingly high push-out rates, and poor attendance continued to be the norm at King High School.

The social and academic contexts illuminated in the preceding paragraphs form the backdrop of my second year as an English teacher at King High. A few short weeks into the 2005–2006 academic term, I recognized that our school was experiencing a drastic decrease in morale, which was evidenced by the cloud of hopelessness cast over many of our students and staff. Although some teachers' pessimistic spirits contributed to our collective demise, I stayed encouraged as our academic standing declined. I devoted more time to creative lesson planning—and commiserated and strategized with a handful of other practitioners who had not yet become jaded. Still, I often contemplated how, if at all, were our students locating comparable sources of refuge.

Taking the Road Less Traveled

In the year leading up to the development of Black Girls United, individuals associated with King High School were frequently discussed in the most derogatory terms. The dominant narrative regarding the school was that its students were aggressive, economically impoverished, and lazy. Moreover, prevailing perceptions of the adult faculty and staff at our school maligned these parties as uncaring and incompetent. Many of the approaches to improving our campus espoused the assumption that something was broken and needed fixing. Usually, individuals blamed learners for our institutional difficulties. In other cases, the culprits were hardworking parents, teachers, or administrators. The trouble with these descriptions is that they, for the most part, reflect the perspectives of *outsiders* and they emphasize reducing deficits rather than cultivating strengths and increasing resources.

As an alumnus of King High and a long-time member of the Slauson District, I had developed an *insider* viewpoint and was privy to the inner workings of the school and surrounding community. I recognized that the overwhelming majority of King High youth contradicted the misconceived notions of those unacquainted with our community of learners. While low-test scores and declining graduation rates frequently overshadowed the true character of these students, our young people held a high level of social responsiveness and sensitivity, intelligence, empathy, and amazing problem-solving skills. However, countless students were feeling disempowered and even victimized by the poor social and academic standing of the school. Amidst their many gifts and talents, resentment and a nagging sense of despair threatened learners' ability to focus on state standards and yearly assessments. Furthermore, in spite of the overabundance of extracurricular programs on campus, in only a handful of spaces did students actually feel empowered to address real and pressing socio-cultural concerns that directly impacted their orientation towards school. Most of our campus organizations engaged students through sports, cheerleading, dance, or the arts.

With these challenges in mind, I sought to create a space at King High that focused on developing student agency. Although I was relatively new to teaching, I had gained popularity for my feminist beliefs and my efforts to design more effective and equitable curriculum in my brief one-year tenure at the school. Moreover, my disapproval of racialized sexist social conditioning was widely acknowledged and respected by both students and faculty. However, this reputation did not directly translate into *girls'* student empowerment in my classes.

As mentioned in Chapter 1, I recognized that various Black girl learners displayed fickle patterns of participation during classroom discussions. In numerous informal encounters with these students, I learned of the limited transformative function of my praxis, as several young women felt negatively positioned by the curriculum. These sentiments typically surfaced during discussions in which we explored the intersectionalities of race and gender politics. Black girls in my classes generally felt uncomfortable engaging in critical analyses of their entangled social identities in the presence of their male-identified peers—who misunderstood the young women's uniquely gendered perspectives and realities. On the contrary, I had developed close, personal relationships with many of my African American girl students—who were assertive, opinionated, and far more self-assured outside of the formal classroom setting. Having firsthand experience of the marginalization that Black girl learners endure in urban schooling spaces, I acknowledged the necessity to create an alternative environment that sparked young Black women's intellectual ardor and encouraged their collective activism.

The Lowdown on Black Girls United

Racialized tropes and public assaults on Black women's character were unsheathed in the schoolyard, classrooms, and hallways at King High School. Members of the school community habitually regarded African American young women as loud, ghetto, and lacking the motivation necessary for high levels of academic success. This narrative was reinforced by the scores of Black girl learners at King High who relentlessly auditioned for our trendy cheerleading and dance teams—yet, were often withdrawn in the classroom. I frequently wondered if these students had a *safe space* on our campus that empowered them through agency-oriented curriculum, grounded in intellectual rigor and critical dialogue. Where could African American girls convene as allies to question the discourse of vilification that disparaged Black women? What vehicle could learners utilize to address the gender stratification, abuse, and powerlessness that they habitually experienced inside and outside of school? Finally, and equally as important, where could young

Black women unite in celebration of their collective knowledge, talents, and accomplishments?

After considerable reflection, I sought to extend the work of Black feminist theorists by creating a critical and culturally responsive (Gay, 2000) student organization that responded to the frustrations African American girl adolescents were experiencing in school and their respective communities. Furthermore, I intended to nurture an environment in which these learners could celebrate Black culture and womanhood. Because Black girls were the sole group of students who publicly expressed discomfort in my class and displayed inconsistent patterns of classroom participation, I felt compelled to intervene and offer an unorthodox safe space for these youth. As I contemplated creating Black Girls United, I considered other programs at King High that targeted specific student populations: a collective designated for Black boy adolescents and a student group organized and operated by Latinx youth were two flourishing programs on campus. Although I believed that Black young men and Latinx learners could have benefitted from additional support services at King, I felt an urgent obligation to intervene on behalf of Black girls who, in my opinion, were crying out for help. By prioritizing the socio-cultural and academic concerns, rights, and empowerment of African American girl learners, Black Girls United was uniquely poised to catalyze individual and collective changes that I hoped would yield sustainable improvements in how these youth experienced urban schooling.

Pedagogical Framework

Black Girls United began in the fall 2005 semester and was sustained through the spring 2007 semester. Each week during lunch, members of BGU utilized critical ethnic literature to investigate and work towards resolving historical and contemporary issues facing African American girls and women. These student-led discussions often resulted in meaningful community activities that emerged organically from our conversations. In sum, our shared objectives were to engender solidarity, self-love, and self-definition through dialogue, reflection, and critical analysis. I hoped that through their participation in Black Girls

United, learners' engagement with and orientation towards school would improve in ways that were conducive to their growth as social beings and their academic success, in general.

In developing the curricular and pedagogical structure of BGU, I relied on the scholarship of Black women practitioners such as bell hooks, Gloria Joseph, and other pioneers who explicitly situated their teaching practice within a Black feminist/womanist politic (e.g., Mary McLeod Bethune and Septima Clark). My (re)articulation of Black feminist pedagogy involved developing a framework that was heavily influenced by these women—although it also responded to the sensibilities of my distinct group of urban Black girls and was informed by my personal experiences as an African American woman in a particular time, location, and sociopolitical context.

There were four key elements of this framework. First, we utilized *critical feminist literature* as the basis for each of our lunchtime, student-led discussions. I had aspirations of BGU members cultivating counter-narratives for their personal lives by reading literature written by Black women and various other women of color that challenged traditional representations of non-White femininity in popular literature and the dominant media. Taking into consideration students' varying skill levels and interests, I introduced participants to an assortment of texts (i.e., narrative literature, expository texts, and poetry). Because BGU was not a required course in which individuals would receive a grade, it was critical that the literature was engaging enough to anchor students' investment in the program. For instance, learners drew on Joan Morgan's (1999) *When Chickenheads Come Home to Roost: My Life as a Hip-Hop Feminist* as a starting ground to critique the misogyny in popular rap lyrics, and together we read about the shame that women of color HIV survivors endure in Stella Luna's (2002) "HIV and Me: The Chicana Version" (BGU class, week 40).

Positioning students as agents of change was a second key feature of the organization. In each discussion, the young women in BGU were challenged to develop practical solutions to the problems we explored in the class. Thus, BGU functioned as an alternative and unorthodox ideological space in which students could explore the dialectic of African American women's oppression and their own activism. Through this dialogue, a process of rearticulation occurred: students' experiences took on new meanings, and some individuals developed an alternative view of themselves and the world (Collins, 2000).

Third, we highlighted *collectivity* in BGU. Anyon (1983) wrote about the importance of young girls of color struggling with and against each other to "imagine what could be" (p. 22). Hence, one of the primary objectives of BGU was to unite African American girl learners as allies so that they could collectively challenge, learn from, and empower one another while reconstructing limiting narratives of Black femininity. Group activities such as community jogs and attending local rallies assisted in reinforcing this sisterhood.

Finally, a strongly *politicized ethic of care* was a key element of my Black feminist pedagogical framework. In keeping with the tradition of Black womanist educators, I strategically performed caring by equipping students with the necessary tools to navigate sociopolitical barriers to self and community empowerment. In this context, caring was "infused with love, humility, passion, and power" and demonstrated by unrelenting displays of personal accountability and collective responsibility (Roseboro & Ross, 2009, p. 36). Chapter Five elucidates in greater detail the Black feminist pedagogical framework outlined in this section, as Black Girls United participants' candid accounts of their involvement in the program provide a microanalysis of the learning environment and the instructional approaches that I employed.

Organizational Structure: Who Joined Black Girls United?

One month before the BGU orientation, I submitted a Constitution to the administration at King High School outlining the mission statement and the requirements for student participants—which mainly emphasized the importance of regular attendance and a commitment to completing the assigned readings. During the planning process, I learned that school clubs and organizations outside of athletics were not allowed to discriminate based on race, ethnicity, or gender. Thus, every learner at King High was eligible to join BGU if they met the criteria outlined in the Constitution. I was not alarmed or dissuaded by this revelation, as I predicted that most non-Black female-identified

King High students would not be interested in a program that featured literature, dialogue, and activities steeped explicitly in the social terrain of African American womanhood. In the weeks leading up to the orientation, I informed students in all five sections of my English classes about the emerging program, and I continued preparing for the orientation meeting that would launch Black Girls United in the following weeks. To acquire a pool of African American girl learners that was representative of the entire student body (including the High Achievers Magnet, Apprenticeship Magnet, and the general education track), two of my students made weekly announcements over the school PA system to publicize the organization to the entire student body.

On November 10, 2005 I co-facilitated the Black Girls United orientation in my classroom during the half-hour lunch period. My longtime friend Chisom, who was pursuing a doctorate in education at a local university, offered to assist with the preparation and facilitation of our inaugural BGU meeting. To set the stage for our assembly, I devised a playlist of contemporary music by women R&B and Hip-Hop pioneers. The signature eccentricities of Jill Scott, Erykah Badu, and Lauryn Hill dominated the soundscape of my classroom, which was conveniently located on the second floor of the main building. Five minutes before the gathering commenced, I sprinted downstairs to redeem several boxes of pizza, which I had arranged to arrive at the central office. The melodic sound of Goapele's *Closer* accompanied me through the hallways and back upstairs to my classroom. I hastily opened the door upon my return, and the sight that I stumbled toward blew me away.

Gazing over the stack of warm pizza boxes in my hands, I observed *over fifty* Black girls' bodies jam-packed into my room like a can of sardines. Students sat at desks, squatted on the floor, and stood anxiously against the long wall in the back of the room. A small group of young women crowded beneath the second doorway and peered into the classroom with obvious trepidation. I grinned from ear to ear at the spectacle. Black Girls United had generated unforeseeable interest, which reified my belief in the organization's profound potential to positively influence the social and academic well-being of African American young women at King High School.

As students devoured the pizza, Chisom and I distributed an informational handout that outlined the primary purpose, objectives, and prerequisites for joining BGU. We reviewed the major components of the program, including (but not limited to) the following:

1. Each week, a team of two students will lead literature-based discussions. All students are expected to complete the readings.
2. Discussions will include a *brief* synopsis of the reading, a statement of the problem, and potential solutions.
3. We will eat potluck style each week. Students may sign-up at the first official meeting *(the following week)*.
4. Some meetings will include guest speakers or special activities.
5. We will vote on a President, Vice President, and Secretary who will assist with organizing and recording our meetings and events.

I had previously decided to vet out the most committed students to preserve my ambition of fostering sisterhood and the development of close, personal relationships through BGU. Therefore, in addition to the criteria outlined above, interested parties were required to submit a typed paragraph the following week, detailing what they hoped to gain from the program and their proposed contributions. I hypothesized that this small task would weed out individuals with tenuous interests.

As such, a total of 27 African American girl learners joined Black Girls United on the following Thursday at lunchtime. Each newly minted BGU participant stapled their declaration of commitment to our bulletin board, which was adorned in bright red, black, and green Afrocentric patterns and prominently positioned on the wall behind my desk. The following statements are examples of BGU members' anticipations:

> Some of the things that I would like to learn from [BGU] are how to be able to present myself as a Black girl in today's society, and learn how to set an example the correct way for the younger generation. I would try to put my all into this club as well as my time. I would also try to make it to every meeting that we have. (Brandy)
>
> My commitment to [BGU] and the members is to show up at every meeting on time. To participate in every activity we have, as well as enjoy myself doing so. Grow with each person in the organization. (Violet)

Despite my best efforts to attract African American girl learners from the general education and High Achievers Magnet populations, the overwhelming majority of the students who joined BGU were learners in the Apprenticeship Magnet, one of two accelerated tracks at King High, and the program in which I taught. Most of the individuals who joined the organization were my students or their friends. Additionally, it is imperative to divulge the involvement of three African American boy-identified learners whose initiation into Black Girls United commenced three months after the program was underway. Each young man met the criteria specified in the informational handout and entered the organization with the understanding that BGU was a space for members to negotiate the various challenges that African American women and girls routinely encountered. I do not doubt that their presence impacted the social and intellectual climate of the space; however, the findings of this study indicated that the young men's contributions did not negatively influence the young women BGU participants.

Methodology: A Critical Race Feminist Auto-ethnography

This research was conducted four years after BGU concluded, and I addressed three pressing questions that emerged from my teaching practice in the organization: (a) In what ways, if any, did Black feminist pedagogy impact the racial/ethnic and gender identities of the young African American women participating in BGU? (b) In what ways, if any, did Black feminist pedagogy influence how the students in BGU understood their identities as young Black women? and (c) From the participants' perspectives, in what ways, if any, did BGU help students negotiate the social and academic terrains of school?

I utilized an auto-ethnographic approach to document the effects of Black feminist pedagogy on the identity development of African American girl learners. Similar to other qualitative methods, auto-ethnography relies heavily on storytelling to assist in the interpretation of social interactions (Alexander, 1999). However, auto-ethnography is distinctive in that through the public exposure of personal narratives, a powerful process of self-investigation occurs, wherein the autobiographical and personal are linked to the cultural and social (Ellis, 2004). As an extension of critical race theory (Solorzano, 1997), critical race feminism complicates the feminist practice of autobiographical storytelling within auto-ethnography through the centering of non-White racialized girls and women's experiences (Delgado Bernal, 2002). This auto-ethnography drew on critical race feminist philosophy to denaturalize Eurocentric notions of femininity within educational research practices. Hence, as African American girl learners authoritatively articulated their differential schooling experiences, the hierarchy of knowledge claims was inverted, and the "multiple layered realities in which Black girls exist" became the focus (Evans-Winters & Esposito, 2010, p. 22).

Data Collection

I employed data triangulation techniques to acquire a diverse range of information about what occurred during the Black Girls United meetings and to determine the degree to which my Black feminist pedagogical framework inspired shifts in the participants' conceptions of their race and gender identities. I included the voices of all 27 girl-identified members of BGU in my analysis of (a) field notes, (b) over 35 hours of classroom video footage during weekly lunchtime meetings, (c) student artifacts,[3] and (d) my Black feminist curriculum (weekly themes, corresponding literature, and lesson plans associated with each meeting). Additionally, I conducted two in-depth, individual interviews with a subgroup of seven participants (see Table 1). I based the selection criteria for interview participants on the length and patterns of student participation in the program. Hence, the young women interviewed in this study were members of BGU for its duration (Fall 2005–Spring 2007) and missed one or no meetings in one month.

I conducted two rounds of interviews with each of the seven-subgroup members. In the first round of interviews, my goal was to ascertain learners' raced-gendered perspectives of their personal and family histories, schooling experiences, and orientation towards school *before* joining Black Girls United. I wondered, what familial and community cultural practices did they find meaningful? What kinds of racist or sexist occurrences did students negotiate in their communities before joining BGU? Lastly, how did the participants describe the social and academic landscape of King High School? In my second round of interviews, I focused on students' recollections of their evolving race and gender identities *within the context* of BGU. I was interested in learning how individuals narrated their involvement in the first year of the program, and if their contributions changed over time. I was also curious about students' association with BGU, and if their immersion in the organization impacted their negotiation of the social and academic barriers that they encountered at King High School. As such, I purposely inquired about the potential of the agency-oriented curriculum in Black Girls United to empower learners with the necessary skills to transgress social and school-related difficulties. Finally, as I mentioned earlier in this chapter, I drew on student interviews to fully recount the features of my Black feminist pedagogical framework. During our conversations, members recalled the organizational and pedagogical structure of the program and shared their viewpoints about the safe harbor of strategies and techniques that they enjoyed during our lunchtime assemblies.

To diversify the sample of interviewees, I considered variations in: (a) age, (b) positions within the school academic tracking system, (c) ethnic background, (d) degree of verbal participation in BGU, (e) relationship with the researcher, and (f) involvement in other school-related extracurricular activities.

Members of Black Girls United varied in *age*, although most learners were in the eleventh or twelfth grades. I was interested in why students volunteered to join the program and hypothesized that participants' initial interest might have varied based on grade level or the number of years an individual attended King High School. Moreover, most of the younger BGU participants had stellar attendance; yet, they were less vocal during meetings. To best assess the *effects* of the Black feminist pedagogical practices that I applied in BGU, I explored whether there was a connection between students' ages and their levels of comfort vocalizing their opinions within the context of our meetings.

Table 1 Description of the interview participants.

Name*	Grade	Track**	Ethnicity	Verbal partici- pation	Relationship with researcher	Additional extracur- ricular activities***
Ashanti	11th & 12th	General Education	African American	Vocal	Student	Yes (mildly active)
Tanya	11th & 12th	Apprenticeship Magnet	Belizean	Vocal	Non-Student	Yes (highly active)
Nia	11th & 12th	Apprenticeship Magnet	African American	Vocal	Non-Student	No (inactive)
Brittney	11th & 12th	Apprenticeship Magnet	African American	Reticent	Non-Student	Yes (highly active)
Lisa	11th & 12th	Apprenticeship Magnet	African American	Vocal	Student	Yes (mildly active)
Kenya	10th & 11th	Apprenticeship Magnet	African American	Reticent	Student	No (inactive)
Erykah	9th & 10th	Apprenticeship Magnet	Belizean	Reticent	Student	Yes (mildly active)

Another important factor that I considered when selecting inter-view participants was members' *position within the school tracking system.* As previously stated, 87 percent of the students in BGU were enrolled in the Apprenticeship Magnet—the program in which I taught. It is critical to mention that the Apprenticeship Magnet was one of two magnet departments at King High, which incorporated grades and standardized test performance as measures to admit potential students. Furthermore, the Apprenticeship Magnet track was designed to help prepare high school youth for a career in teaching. Because this is both a very specific and narrow group of individuals, the focal interview-ees did not adequately represent the King High School student body. Nonetheless, I included one student who was in the general education program, in an attempt to address this shortcoming.

The third variable in choosing the subgroup of interviewees was *ethnic background.* Although all BGU members self-identified as Black or African American, the young women constituted a pan-ethnic group. Some Black Girls United members were of Belizean, Brazilian, or Jamaican ancestry, spoke a variety of languages and dialects, and held different immigration and citizenship statuses. Such varied ethnic and cultural identities contributed to BGU members' wide-ranging perspectives, which greatly enriched the conversations and writing that took place within the program. Hence, including an ethnically diverse sample of participants for this study was essential to determining the effects, if any, of Black feminist pedagogy on the racial and ethnic identities of the participants.

In deciding on which students to include in this study, I chose a unique blend of young women based on *the degree to which each individual verbally participated* in Black Girls United. Initially, the program was created to provide a *safe space* for African American girl students to share their collective voice and wisdom. After reflecting on our class meetings (via videotape and field notes), I discovered that BGU members could be divided into two distinct groups: learners who spoke at almost every meeting, and participants who rarely uttered a word. In order to uncover the effects, if any, of Black feminist pedagogy on students' racial/ethnic and gender identities, it was important to include the opinions of all members—particularly those who were most reticent. I wondered if the silence of some students implied that they were uncomfortable sharing their thoughts and opinions in BGU? If so, what do their actions imply about the usefulness of the space, and the effectiveness of Black feminist pedagogy in general? Interviews served as a useful data source to answer these questions.

The fifth variable in selecting the subgroup of seven members was students' *relationships with the researcher.* As detailed earlier in the chapter, many of the learners in Black Girls United were my students in my English classes. It was necessary for me to be transparent about my positionality to assess the effect of Black feminist pedagogy on these youth's racial/ethnic and gender identities, and differentiate the extent to which my relationships with members influenced the findings of this research. Thus, in determining the participants for this study, I selected three individuals whom I had formerly taught, and three students who I knew by association. I strived for a balance of including members that I knew intimately and participants with whom I was less attached, which was critical to determining how my demeanor and connections with students factored into why individuals joined the program. Moreover, gathering participants across the spectrum of *relationships with the researcher* produced reliable data about how many Black girl learners enjoyed the organization and the bearing of Black feminist curricula on their social and educational identities.

One of the sub-questions of this study was to determine, from the participants' perspectives, in what ways, if any, did Black Girls United help students cope with the *social* and *academic* terrains of school? To address this question and best determine the degree to which Black feminist pedagogy assisted learners in navigating the schooling process, it was imperative that the participants involved in the study represented the full spectrum of the members of the organization. Hence, I included individuals who, at the inception of the program, were highly active, mildly active, and fairly inactive[4] in school. Thus, *involvement in other school-related extracurricular activities* was the sixth variable for selecting the representative sample of seven former members.

Data Analysis

Data triangulation techniques were essential to acquiring a varied range of information about what occurred in Black Girls United, an in-depth understanding of how the participants made sense of these interactions, and to enable a convergence of conclusions across multiple data sources (McMillan, 2016). Hence, the BGU curriculum, field notes, videotaped meetings, interviews, and artifacts were all sources of potential data. The knowledge that these sources contained were transcribed, organized, coded, and systematically reviewed to become the eventual data that substantiated my assertions regarding the research site and study participants.

To effectively analyze my data sources, I used Critical Discourse Analysis (CDA) (Fairclough, 1995) and grounded theory (Strauss & Corbin, 1998). Fairclough describes CDA as a three-dimensional process that includes, "analysis of (spoken or written) language texts, analysis of discourse practice (processes of text production, distribution, and consumption) and analysis of discursive events as instances of sociocultural practice" (p. 2). As such, micro (i.e., text syntax, rhetoric), meso (i.e., power relations in production and consumption), and macro-level (i.e., intertextual understandings, societal currents) interpretations of discourse provide a system by which one may read into the academic, social, political, and ideological meanings of discourse data (Strauss & Corbin, 1998). Thus, in my analysis of data, I looked closely at the specific structures of text, as well as the socio-political systems and contexts in which they emerged. Specifically, I was attentive to how the discursive exchanges within Black Girls United reproduced or resisted dominant notions of Black femininity.

Combined with Critical Discourse Analysis, I applied grounded theory as an inductive, bottom-up approach to analyzing my corpus of data. Strauss and Corbin (1998) underscore the importance for researchers to "acquire a way of thinking about data and the world in which they live ... to be able to easily move from what they see and hear and to raise that to the level of the abstract, and then to turn around again and move back to the level of data" (p. 8). Hence, I started on the *ground* with the data, which inductively evolved into more abstract phenomena. This method of analysis was critical to my study because although I was open to concepts and patterns that emerged during the analytical process, I did not presume an objective stance. I then integrated theoretical constructs—or *abstraction*—into the analysis as a means of accountability to my Black girl learner research subjects, and the conditions in which they lived.

To reduce and analyze the data that I acquired throughout this study, I labeled phenomena, discovered emerging categories, conducted a cross-comparison of classifications, developed hypotheses and theoretical perspectives derived from the data, and checked for confirming and disconfirming evidence for each assertion. Upon the conclusion of the data analysis process, I acquired a profound understanding of the following questions: How did African American girl students narrate their social and academic struggles in Black Girls United? What happened *after* youth recounted the obstacles in their lives? Was there a *shift* in how young Black women conceptualized their race and gender identities? Lastly, did the members report a change in their social and academic behaviors as a result of their participation in the program?

Gettin' Schooled: Positionality and Practitioner Research

I entered into this project four years after I parted ways with King High School to pursue my doctorate degree. There were great possibilities in transitioning from the community to the academy: I had the opportunity to contest the longstanding popular and scholarly narratives regarding the academic underachievement and cultural subjectivities of urban African American young women. Additionally, I could potentially influence the national debate on best teaching practices in urban schools and inform the preparation of future K–12 public school educators. To be candid, moreover, I had an unabashedly *homegurl* mentality when I embarked on this journey. Not to be confused with the cliché loud talkin', self-indulgent, anti-intellectual Black woman caricature that is plastered across American television, cinema, and social media platforms—a *homegurl*, by my definition, is the antithesis of this melodramatic portrayal. She is self-defining. She is resilient. She is driven by an intense love for family and community. Through her lens, a formal education is futile if it does not serve the interests of those who are most marginalized in our society. Essentially, a *homegurl* values education beyond the means of employability; it is a vehicle for self-actualization *and* civic responsibility. I entered my doctoral program with the ambitious intention of using my intellectual capital as such. Regrettably, two years into my studies, I realized my vision had somehow gone awry.

After completing coursework, the next course of action was to establish my dissertation study's design. I was certain of the "what" of the investigation: I was going to research the role of Black feminist pedagogy in the racial/ethnic and gender identity development of students in Black Girls United. Furthermore, I was interested in how shifts in individuals' racial and gender identities influenced their orientation toward school. The unanswered question was, with what means would I ascertain this information? Consequently, I ran into one of the greatest challenges in my doctoral program: *the methods conundrum*. Graduate students faced immense pressure to engage in solely quantitative or mixed methods research. Pressure emanated from various sources, including distinguished faculty members and fellow students. It was considered universal knowledge, part of the "not-so-hidden curriculum," that quantitative studies are often perceived as more reliable and generalizable as specified by classic scientific research standards.

As an impressionable, budding scholar concerned with the marketability of my research in the academic economy, I obsessed over whether my dissertation would rival extant educational literature, my ability to acquire fellowship opportunities, and the degree to which my methodological choices could influence eventual job opportunities. I concluded that a mixed methods study would increase my chances of success at all three of my aforementioned anxieties. It was official; my *researcher* identity had emerged. Success in the academy—as measured by White hegemonic ways of knowing and doing—was equated with my ability to achieve wealth and superstardom as a university professor. The sociopolitical concerns and interests of research participants were overshadowed by my personal crusade for economic and professional gains. I was rapidly losing sight of my *homegurl* sensibilities; they had become a faint glimmer at the end of a long, windy tunnel.

The challenges I faced negotiating the competing dualities of my *homegurl* and *researcher* identities is a common struggle among scholars of color. Universities have historically existed as racialized, cultured, gendered, classed, and highly political spaces—and non-White graduate students have endured various instances of marginality at the crossroads of our multiple identities. Dillard (2008) documents this phenomenon and encourages researchers to *re-member* the "things that we've learned to forget" (p. 89). She calls for individuals to recall racial/ cultural, spiritual, and/or political expertise to guide us in conducting ethical, empowering research. As Dillard explains, a principled and liberatory approach to research necessitates that educators draw on the Spirit within—namely, the concrete experiences of our everyday lives that serve as the basis of our current wisdom, and the ways in which we make sense of the world (Dillard, 2002, 2006). Embodying these experiences, Dillard purports, is key to working in concert *with* research participants, and ultimately engaging in the kind of transformative education that serves the greatest good. For me, this meant "wandering back into a familiar context" (p. 89) and reclaiming my purpose in the academy.

I stumbled upon Dillard's concept of *re-membering* through an experience I had with a former member of Black Girls United. As I developed my dissertation research proposal, I met with a handful of students to gauge their willingness to participate in the study. One student, Ashanti, experienced a tragic accident in her family just one week prior to our meeting. Her cousin was murdered in a drive-by shooting while standing outside of an acquaintance's home. On the day we met for lunch, my intentions were to briefly check in with Ashanti regarding her emotional state and then proceed with the business of my dissertation. With pen and notebook in hand, I was in full *researcher* mode when I met her in the parking lot. The original motivation behind our meeting was lost when I looked into her eyes; she was still visibly shaken, and undeniably heartbroken.

My lunch with Ashanti ultimately served a much higher purpose than to advance my research objectives. In that meeting, she and I embodied Black feminist praxis as we explored the dialectic of our oppression and our activism as African American women. We spoke about love. We shared stories about death and familial cycles of pathology. We disclosed our fears and shared feelings of powerlessness. And we challenged each other to look to Spirit to reclaim our agency in times of sadness and despair. *Re-membering* these stories and cultural experiences with Ashanti reified my purpose for entering into academia: to use education as a liberatory tool to subvert the oppressive conditions under which many urban African American girls exist. The systematic ways in which schools disengage young Black women through de-humanizing pedagogies, racial and socio-economic isolation, and limited academic support exerts tremendous influence on these youth's ability to realize their full potential as young adults. Ashanti's cousin was a disturbingly frightening reminder of this fact.

Later that afternoon, I concluded that my *homegurl* and *researcher* identities were not adversaries. Admittedly, the *researcher* in me was self-serving, pushy, and determined—however, this state of being also equipped me with the necessary knowledge and adeptness to navigate the competitive, alienating world of academia. My *homegurl* sensibility, on the other hand, functioned as a constant reminder to the *researcher* of the unyielding passion from which my scholarship emerged, and my commitment to continually engage in work that is in service of others. My mind, body, and spirit were fully reengaged in the dissertation process when I recognized the transformative potential of oscillating between these two dispositions. My challenge was to develop an innovative and empirically sound methodological framework representing the voices of participants with dignity and truthfulness.

Practitioner Research and Related Consequences

As a teacher-researcher, I was acutely aware of my positionality and political interests throughout this study. Because I had researched the high school I had formerly attended and at the school where I previously taught, I gained an acute awareness of the micropolitics of the research site. Moreover, I also accept that I had certain preconceived notions about the focal students and the school site itself. Over the course of six years, my role with several of the BGU members evolved tremendously—I was no longer simply their teacher. Over time, I became a mentor, confidant, and friend to many of the young women. While these conditions may have skewed my data collection (e.g., participants altering behaviors and interview responses based on my positionality) and posed a validity threat, I feel it is essential to recognize them for the sake of revealing possible biases. Good qualitative researchers have a heightened awareness of how our personal experiences, social identities, and the ideologies we carry innately sway the findings of our studies. Engaging in critical examinations of these subjectivities adds to the credibility of our scholarship (McMillan, 2016). Moreover, my *insider* access to King High School and the Black Girls United participants created a tremendous responsibility on my part to capture youth voices with depth and precision. Accordingly, I utilized numerous data sources and member checking throughout to ensure that I presented the findings accurately and fairly.

For instance, I conducted two sets of semi-structured, in-depth interviews with each of the seven participants in the representative sample. Because several years had passed since students participated in BGU, I provided participants with our reading list, as well as selected curricular materials during interviews to assist in their memory recall, and enhance the reliability of participants remembering what took place. In situating this methodology within a critical race feminist theoretical framework, I was most interested in the relationship between the learners' individual and nuanced experiences, and the broader social, cultural, and political frames from which they emerged. Thus, I aimed to analyze how the schooling encounters of the interviewees had been shaped by the intersections of various structures of domination—as opposed to exploring them as isolated events. Furthermore, a semi-structured, open-ended protocol created opportunities for me to ask core questions while maintaining the freedom to continue with follow-up questions when unexpected topics emerge during the interview (Brenner, 2006). I had intended for participants to oscillate between modes of informant and respondent as they made meaning of their own lives and experiences. I am hopeful that this methodology enabled my Black girl learners to *realize* themselves in one way or another throughout the interview process.

Finally, it is also imperative to articulate how my personal history and experiences as a Black woman have influenced the purpose of this research and the methods employed. Locating my realities within a Black feminist frame, I recognize the countless ways in which interlocking forms of race, class, and gender oppression stifle African American women's full expression of humanity. I relied on narrative, qualitative methods to investigate the potential of Black feminist pedagogy because it is particularly effective at capturing the distinctive standpoints and understandings of the researcher and the participants—thereby providing a rich contextual analysis from which new theory emerges or pre-existing theory is supported (Maxwell, 1996). As such, there were two primary reasons for conducting this inquiry. One aim was to depathologize urban Black girls by analyzing the conditions of their racialized and gendered oppression. The second objective of this study was to unearth the pedagogical strategies that cultivated empowered social identities and intellectual curiosity among the BGU participants. The research presented in *Engendering #BlackGirlJoy* is novel, as I explore the means by which the goals above are accomplished through an oppositional space of existence *within* the context of a school site.

In conducting this study, I was concerned with shedding light on my former students' lived experiences and the intricate human realities that Black women carry as racialized women. Thus, given the focus on the rich counternarratives of these Black girl adolescents and the goal of understanding how Black feminist pedagogy impacted their race and gender identities, the growth that my girls and I experienced together was as significant as the insight gained through the telling of our stories. I am forever indebted to the young Black women who narrated their lives fearlessly, and in exacting detail—without a trace of self-pity and boundless aspirations for their blooming social and educative lives.

Questions for Deeper Engagement

1. Practitioner research situates educators as *scholar-activists*, which challenges the inertia and unwieldiness of educational reform. How does your school site make meaning of data on student and teacher performance? To what degree do these data challenge existing practices and inspire teachers to take risks in improving student outcomes?

2. Identify a gap between your present practice and where you want to be. How might you engage in research as a professional growth opportunity? Imagine taking up a systematic inquiry to strengthen your skills as a reflective practitioner, gather information, and understand phenomena at your school site more thoroughly. How would you begin?

Notes

1 All persons, programs, and locations named here are pseudonyms.

2 As a consequence of low-test scores, LAUSD initiated mandates that required teachers at King High to revamp the curriculum. The new curriculum heavily prioritized test preparation, and in effect, was highly disengaging for most students.

3 Artifacts included tangible objects that were emblematic of a shift in identity development, such as written documents and digital media.

4 For the purpose of this study, students who were *highly active* participated in two or more extracurricular activities outside of BGU; students who were *mildly active* participated in one additional extracurricular activity outside of BGU; students who were *inactive* did not participate in any additional activities.

References

Alexander, B. K. (1999). Performing culture in the classroom: An instructional (auto) ethnography. *Text and Performance Quarterly, 19*, 307–331.

Anyon, J. (1983). Intersections of gender and class: Accommodation and resistance by working-class and affluent females to contradictory sex-role ideologies. In S. Walker & L. Barton (Eds.), *Gender, class and education* (pp. 19–38). London, UK: Falmer.

Brenner, M. E. (2006). Interviewing in educational research. In J. L. Green, G. Camilli, & P. B. Elmore (Eds.), *Handbook of complementary methods in education research* (pp. 357–370). Mahwah, NJ: Lawrence Erlbaum.

Collins, P. H. (2000). *Black feminist thought: Knowledge, consciousness, and the politics of empowerment* (2nd ed.). New York, NY: Routledge.

Delgado Bernal, D. (2002). Critical race theory, Latino critical theory, and critical raced-gendered epistemologies: Recognizing students of color as holders and creators of knowledge. *Qualitative Inquiry, 8*(1), 105–126.

Dillard, C. B. (2002). Walking ourselves back home: The education of teachers with/in the world. *Journal of Teacher Education, 53*(5), 383–392.

Dillard, C. B. (2006). When the music changes, so should the dance: cultural and spiritual considerations in paradigm "proliferation." *International Journal of Qualitative Studies, 19*(1), 59–76.

Dillard, C. B. (2008). Re-membering culture: Bearing witness to the spirit of identity in research. *Race and Ethnicity in Education, 11*(1), 87–93.

Ellis, C. (2004). *The ethnographic I: A methodological novel about teaching and doing autoethnography.* Walnut Creek, CA: AltaMira.

Evans-Winters, V. E., & Esposito, J. (2010). Other people's daughters: Critical race feminism and Black girls' education. *Educational Foundations, 24*(1/2), 11–24.

Fairclough, N. (1995). *Critical discourse analysis: The critical study of language.* New York, NY: Longman.

Gay, G. (2000). *Culturally responsive teaching: Theory, research, and practice.* New York: Teachers College Press.

Luna, S. (2002). HIV and me: The Chicana version. In D. Hernandez & B. Rehman (Eds.), *Colonize this! Young women of color on today's feminism* (pp. 71–84). Emeryville, CA: Seal Press.

Maxwell, J. A. (1996). *Qualitative research design: An interactive approach.* Thousand Oaks, CA: Sage.

McMillan, J. (2016). *Educational research: Fundamentals for the consumer* (7th edition). Boston, MA: Pearson.

Morgan, J. (1999). *When chickenheads come home to roost: My life as a hip-hop feminist.* New York, NY: Simon & Schuster.

Roseboro, D. L., & Ross, S. N. (2009). Care-sickness: Black women educators, care theory, and a hermeneutic of suspicion. *Educational Foundations, 23*(3/4), 19–40.

Solorzano, D. (1997). Images and words that wound: Critical race theory, racial stereotyping, and teacher education. *Teacher Education Quarterly, 24*(3), 5–19.

Strauss, A., & Corbin, J. M. (1998). *Basics of qualitative research: Techniques and procedures for developing grounded theory.* Thousand Oaks, CA: Sage.

"When I was in the 11th grade I couldn't ditch yo class…I didn't want to, cuz we were doin' real shit. Plus, I couldn't. It was first period, and you woke me up every morning!....But there were times in the 12th grade when I'd go to Ashley's [a pseudonym] class instead of my English class. But that's cuz her teacher was cool...He used to be like, 'yo, if you gon' be in here, you gon' do work'. So, I'd get my notebook out!....I'd rather do his work than work for the class that I was in…cuz it was challenging…and I figured I would need to know that shit for college!"

~Ashanti

Invisibility and Hyper-Visibility: Perceptions of Black Girls in an Urban School

Introduction: A Hard Knock Life

Pac[1] said, "We ain't meant to survive, cuz it's a set up. And even tho you're fed up, you gotta keep your head up." So many of my girls are struggling to keep their heads up—which I understand—considering all the pain that they endure. And I'm certain I only know the half of it. Some [students] are so stressed out. Aged beyond their years. At 15 and 16 years old, some of them look older than me! They are tired, but resilient. Pac was right, "they ain't meant to survive." It seems that prosperity and happiness are privileges—rewards that only a lucky few low-income Black girls manage to procure after the long and grueling hazing process that we call life. Relentless struggle is what these students have been conditioned to expect as young Black women. With the odds stacked against them, a rough existence is perceived as normal, natural, and unjust. I've encountered these sentiments in their written assignments. Today, I was reminded of that truth. It's a "hard knock life"[2] for Black girls. (Journal 1, Entry 6, p. 17)

I scribbled the opening field note on a Thursday afternoon, during my sixth-period conference. It was the day of the first Black Girls United meeting, and I was mentally and physically exhausted. Earlier that afternoon, over 50 young women had flocked to my classroom during the lunch break, each hoping for entry into the highly anticipated program. We covered several important topics during that gathering, including the primary objectives of the organization and the requirements for joining BGU. Notwithstanding the empowering, feel-good energy that saturated my classroom during our assembly, I was distracted by a statement that one student expressed in the final moments of our meeting. After I covered the logistics of the organization, I asked individuals to share their perceptions of the present state of Black womanhood. The answers varied: Black women were "invisible" (Daniella, BGU Class, Week 1); Black women were survivors of oppression and domestic abuse, and a large majority of Africa's daughters were "trying to rediscover their *queendom*" (Nia, BGU Class, Week 1). The last student to respond was Chrisette, an eleventh-grader who rested against a stool in the back of the room. After listening to her peers' replies, Chrisette stood tall and asserted:

> We are the underdogs. Everything we have, society tries to take from us—to keep us on the bottom. They don't want us to win. We have to protect our children, our families … our education. But we fighters. And some of us fight so hard, we die tryin' to make it to the top. You know, those are the statistics. The rest of us just keep fightin'. But some of us … most of us … *end up defeated.* (BGU class, Week 1)

Chrisette's comment sparked numerous nods of agreement from her peers. As the bell rang, I informed the group that we would begin the following week's meeting with a reflection on Chrisette's observation. Later that day, during my sixth-period conference, I thought deeply about the events that had transpired in our meeting. Students' interpretations of the condition of Black womanhood were saddening. Resilience was a common theme; however, the concept of African American women's imminent defeat was similarly prevalent. As a 24-year-old Black woman and alumni of King High School, I had experienced (and was still negotiating) many of the oppressive social conditions that my students highlighted in our first discussion. Yet, I was bewildered and disheartened by the number of young women at our meeting who shared feelings of impending defeat as teenagers; as a school-aged girl, I had never grappled with such thoughts. Therefore, I was gravely concerned about the schooling trajectories and life prospects of the Black Girls United prospects. That afternoon I wrote, "*Why do so many of these girls believe that they are destined to fail? And how can I possibly expect them to give a damn about school, if they are convinced that failure is lurking around the corner?*" In the months that followed, and throughout the two-year program, the members of Black Girls United answered the questions that I posed in my journal after our first meeting. During our weekly lunchtime sessions, BGU participants named their realities as urban African American young women, and resiliently "struggled with and against each other" to puncture the profoundly embedded, dominant social discourses and ideologies that influenced their collective understanding of Black femininity (Sears, 2010, p. 22).

The goal of this inquiry was to determine the effects of Black feminist pedagogy on the race and gender identities of the members of BGU. I also sought to unearth how BGU aided learners' negotiation of the *social* and *academic* terrains of school. To address my first and second sub-questions, I disentangled the factors—both inside and outside of school—that shaped the ways that the participants understood themselves as racialized and gendered beings, *before* joining the program. Furthermore, it was imperative to determine how students interpreted and coped with the social and academic cultures of King High School. I utilized all five data sources in my analysis: (a) two sets of semi-structured, in-depth interviews with a representative research sample of seven former BGU members; (b) 35 hours of video recordings from BGU classes; (c) my curriculum (i.e., student work, thematic units, lesson plans, and corresponding literature); (d) two years of field notes from in-class and out-of-class interactions; and (e) student artifacts.

It is critical to note that I did not have access to interviews with participants, artifacts, student work, or video of BGU members *prior* to their participation with Black Girls United. As such, I relied on data from the first five weeks of the program to investigate how the young women narrated their social and educational lives before joining the organization. During the early weeks of BGU, our literature and class discussions explicitly focused on how the cultural shapings of racialized gender norms played out in students' lives as urban African

American adolescents. Furthermore, the bulk of my analysis draws on interviews with students that I conducted after the program concluded, video recordings from class sessions, and artifacts. All three of these information sources provided *firsthand* accounts of learners' interpretations of the numerous factors contributing to their race and gender identity development, leading up to their association with Black Girls United. Alternatively, my field notes and BGU curriculum were useful to elucidate my interpretations of the participants' race and gender ideologies, which I compared to the students' accounts.

An analysis of the data has illuminated Black Girls United members' initial perspectives of themselves as politicized beings. The findings revealed that the participants had a powerful, collective recognition of their status as a multiply subordinated group. While the objective of my research was to examine race and gender as separate entities, I have discovered that for BGU youth, race and gender were deeply entangled, and rarely teased apart in discussions around identity. This finding reinforces the scholarship of Muhammad and Dixson (2008), who identify an "indivisible oneness of racialized gender experiences and feminized racial experiences" among high school aged Black girls (p. 176). The African American young women in BGU both support and extend the authors' findings. In the context of this study, race and gender were also inextricably tied to *class*. Multiple sources of data have underscored Black Girls United participants' intersectional analysis, which speaks truth to power by naming and addressing the simultaneity of race, gender, and class oppression that the young women encountered in their daily lives.

The subordination that BGU youth combatted manifested in two distinct ways: the members felt a general sense of *invisibility*—and at the other end of the spectrum, *hyper-visibility*—resulting from various socially denigrating experiences in their communities and at King High School. A plethora of Black feminist scholarship has unearthed both the historical patterns as well as the contemporary means by which society disenfranchises African American women (Collins, 2000; Davis, 1983; hooks, 1984). The students in BGU have a similar testimony—their general sense of *invisibility* was attributed to the prolonged deprivation of critical resources in their communities (e.g., economic capital) and at school (i.e., motivated teachers). A common thread across data sources included the perception that poor Black women are at the bottom of society's race-gender hierarchy. As a consequence, the desires and needs of African American girls in economically under-resourced neighborhoods are disregarded—rendering these adolescents both unvoiced and unseen.

Alternatively, ubiquitous messages about Black women's inferiority throughout U.S. popular media resulted in BGU participants' shared consciousness of their hyper-visibility. Extant Black feminist scholarship has well-documented portrayals of African American women as anti-intellectual, aggressive, and inherently sexual in mainstream television, film, and music (Harris-Perry, 2011; Morgan, 1999). The dehumanizing interactions with teachers and peers (i.e., slanderous discourse about Black girl learners, and teachers' low academic expectations) at King High School reinforced the specific, fixed stylization of Black women and girls in the mass media. In sum, the participants of Black Girls United experienced extreme alienation as a consequence of being inundated with stereotypical depictions of themselves—which posed a tremendous threat to youth's self-concepts, moral standing, and perceived intellectual capacities.

The most prominent feature of Black Girls United students' intersecting race, class, and gender identities was the dialectical relationship between their observed *invisibility* and *hyper-visibility*. However, on fleeting occasions participants felt inspired in their communities and at King High School. I refer to these instances as *outliers*, which I have grouped into two categories: (a) *protective mechanisms* employed by parents and guardians, and (b) *small serendipities* at King High School. Several BGU members engaged in resilient social and academic behaviors, which they often attributed to the various *protective mechanisms* that their parents and guardians applied. For instance, the participants reported that family members worked multiple jobs and provided rides to and from school to ensure their children's safety. From the learners' perspectives, the purpose of these protective mechanisms was to increase BGU participants' access to the critical material resources previously discussed (e.g., economic capital), or to support students' academic well-being.

Additionally, there were several *small serendipities* at King High School, which similarly functioned as empowering outliers. For example, some students in Black Girls United reported joining extra-curricular school activities "on a whim" or simply "falling into" academic enrichment programs at the urging of caring teachers or administrators. Several of these programs and organizations inculcated in students a sense of intellectual satisfaction, racial pride, and enhanced self-esteem. Moreover, connections with a few committed faculty members at King High (e.g., teachers and college counselors) inspired youth to stay focused on their academic pursuits; these trusted faculty members also served as a "listening ear" when the young women in BGU needed to vent about problems at home and school. Together, these *small serendipities* were the result of students' perceived good fortune and functioned as distractions from the dehumanizing schooling conditions that they encountered regularly.

Sadly, the empowering *outliers* in BGU members' communities and at King High School were not influential enough to subvert the abundant negative messages students received in those same spaces. As such, Black Girls United youth participated in everyday acts of oppositional resistance against their perceived race, class, and gender subordination. Similar to past research about Black girl learners' defiance in educational contexts, BGU students' behaviors were generally intentional, complex, and socially situated (Fordham, 1993). Moreover, resistance among BGU participants aligns with Robinson and Ward's (1991) concept of *resistance for liberation* and *resistance for survival*. The authors describe *resistance for liberation* as behaviors that serve a higher purpose of individual and community uplift, whereas *resistance for survival* often involves self-defeating or destructive activity. The following sections further explicate these findings into four distinct categories: (a) the multiple phenomena that contributed to BGU students' feelings of *invisibility*, (b) how ubiquitous messages of African American women's inferiority resulted in participants' sense of *hyper-visibility*, (c) the socially and academically empowering school and community *outliers*, and (d) learners' diverse methods of *resistance*.

Invisibility

Hood Life: A Social Ecology of "Less Than"

Andrea (facilitator):	[Poses question to the class] What's the first word that comes to mind when you think about your community?
Chloe:	[Raises hand] Poor.
Andrea (facilitator):	Umm, ok, can you elaborate on that [Chloe]?
Chloe:	Yeah, ok [pauses] … we don't have a lot. Of *anything*, really. Not in my neighborhood. Money, clothes, food. You know, a lot of people don't even have enough food to get by. *We* cool tho'. My family's getting by. You know, folks in the hood just have less. *Less than* everybody else.
Andrea (facilitator):	Ok, good. So, people in the hood automatically have less than everybody else. Ok. Why? What do you think … well, what's the cause of the poverty in your community? And in the hood in general?
Tanisha:	[Interjects] It's like this, [pauses] basically, we ain't *got shit*, cuz we *ain't shit!*
Andrea (facilitator):	Says who?!
Tanisha:	*Everybody.* [Looks around for approval from the class] Don't even front! *Society* says so! [Side chatter ensues, and some students respond with 'yep']
Ms. Lane:	Do *you* believe that you 'ain't shit'?
Tanisha:	*Heck naw!* [Laughter]

The excerpt above represents a glimpse of our third Black Girls United meeting, which was facilitated by an eleventh-grade student named Andrea. For homework, the members of BGU were required to read an article by Taigi Smith (2002) entitled, *What Happens When Your Hood is the Last Stop on the White Flight Express*? The purpose of Smith's reading was twofold: (a) to highlight the beauty and cultural wealth of students' respective communities, and (b) to discuss how community revitalization projects often lead to the displacement of families of color, and single mothers particularly. Smith's reading familiarized students with this process; the author's personal story of gentrification in the Mission District of San Francisco provided the backdrop against which students could compare the progression of gentrification in the neighborhoods surrounding King High School. When Andrea opened the discussion by asking individuals to share the "first thing that comes to mind" when they think about their communities, the conversation moved in a surprising direction.

Rather than reflecting on the advantages of living in urban districts that are teeming with cultural affluence, students illuminated— and subsequently critiqued—the scarcity of economic capital in their respective communities. Then, Chloe's assertion that "folks in the hood have *less than* everybody else" opened up Pandora's Box. Individuals went on to describe their neighborhoods as "dirty," "depressing," and "crowded." For many participants, a by-product of living in economically impoverished urban areas meant that individuals could not adequately access the resources to meet their basic needs in shelter, employment, and health. For instance, an eleventh-grader named Kennisha revealed that the inaccessibility of fresh, organic produce in her neighborhood was a major obstacle to the physical health and well-being of individuals in her community. She declared, "Me and my family have to leave South LA to grocery shop because all of the stores around here have old, spoiled food—the leftovers that they not gon' send to the stores in the rich areas! But they could care less about *us*! We don't matter. So they just throw us the scraps!" Kennisha's comment reaffirms Tanisha's sentiment that people in low-income communities are disposable to the larger society. Such circumstances prohibit individuals from acquiring the resources to sustain themselves and their families adequately.

In my first set of individual interviews with a sub-sample of seven former BGU students, the participants discussed the centrality of race *and* gender in the alienation of individuals residing in economically under-resourced communities. During my conversation with a member named Tanya, we discussed her awareness of racial and gender discrimination as a student attending King High. As she recounted the subordination that she navigated at the intersections of her entangled identities, Tanya asserted:

> Well, before I joined [Black Girls United] I used to feel like nobody cares about poor *minorities*. Especially *poor Black women*. Like, for us … poverty is a cycle because racism and sexism keeps us from getting jobs. White people can escape the poverty, because they'll get hired before we do. And

men—you know—they *always* gonna be above women in our society. You know what I mean? But as a Black woman, it's like … we're *stuck,* you know? We're forced to live in crowded inner cities. In apartments and projects where we're stacked on top of each other. And you got single moms havin' to live that way too! Squished! Like, that's why *so many* Black women have a "I don't care" mentality. Like, what the hell am I supposed to do?! Because in order to *do better* you have to be *given better,* and put in better situations. And that's why so many of us have just given up. You feel me? Cuz' we need to be put in better situations. But, we don't have access to better situations. (Tanya, Interview #1, October 26, 2012)

The notion that the deprivation of low-income Black women has pushed individuals into a state of powerlessness was a common theme amongst Black Girls United students. On many occasions—as I reviewed video of BGU classes, interviews with students, field notes, and artifacts—the Black Girls United participants regarded being poor, Black, and girl adolescents as a trifecta of suffering. During my interview with Nia, she described why it is particularly challenging for low-income Black women to maintain a sense of dignity in the face of interlocking oppressions. Prior to joining BGU, Nia briefly attended Pierson High School, located in an upper middle-class suburb roughly 40 minutes from King High. In our conversation, she recalled an experience in which a White male student referred to her as "ghetto" during a class discussion. In the following quote, Nia articulates why the White-identified male student's hurling of the racist and gendered epithet was one of the most dehumanizing experiences of her lifetime as an adolescent. Additionally, Nia explains how his comment reinforced her outlook on the status of Black women in the larger society:

When he called me ghetto, I learned that being a poor Black girl is the worst thing to be! Cuz' you're not just poor, or just Black, or just female. You're *all three!* And to call somebody ghetto is the worst! Especially if you're called a "ghetto Black girl." And, that's how I felt before I became a part of [Black Girls United]. Like, you can call me a lot of things, but as a Black girl, *don't you dare* call me ghetto! Because it means that you're *nothing.* Not smart, not beautiful. You are classless. I mean, he said it like he was disgusted. "You are a ghetto Black girl." *You are nothing.* Like, "I don't even see you. I don't even recognize your existence." It was really degrading. After someone calls you that, what do you do? How do you respond to that? Like, what can you *really* do about it? I was flabbergasted. (Nia, Interview #1, October 12, 2012)

During my second interview with Nia, we spoke in greater detail about her understanding of the socio-political location of low-income Black women, *before* joining Black Girls United. This member checking was useful in verifying an important finding from her previous interview—that is, being poor, Black, and girl adolescents was the lowest notch inscribed on the social ladder. As I encouraged Nia to articulate her stance further, she proclaimed, "I think that if you're poor and Black, nobody cares. If you're a poor Black woman, you're *really* in trouble!" (Interview #2, December 8, 2012).

Although Nia's sentiment frequently appeared in conversations about how African American women are positioned in the larger society, the participants' sense of invisibility was also at the center of many discussions regarding students' academic experiences at King High School. Young Black women were the majority population among girl adolescents at King; however, many of these youth felt overlooked and alienated on campus. In essence, students' interactions with apathetic and unenthusiastic teachers at King High School mirrored the invisibility that youth experienced in their neighborhoods (and in the larger society, in general).

Invisibility at King High

In my second interview with a former BGU student named Tanya, I asked, "What motivated you to attend [King]?" Without hesitating she replied, "I'm not gonna lie, what is every kid who attended [King] High feeling about school?" [Imitating her peers] "Oh my God, they filmed [Take Me Out to the Ball Game] here." Like, that was my *only* motivation [laughing]. And then you know, sports and basketball. (Tanya, Interview #2, December 22, 2012)

Tanya went on to describe King's notorious reputation for producing well-known college and professional athletes, and the history of the school as the "go to" location for urban blockbuster films. Her response was predictable, as I previously posed the same question to six other former BGU members, and their reactions were comparable to Tanya's. In my interviews, students provided three specific impetuses for enrolling in King High School: it was the safest local school, King High was their designated home school, and the school had a longstanding reputation for housing the city's "cool kids." After interviewing each of the seven participants from my representative research sample—and as a former King High student *and* teacher, I understood why the school's academic reputation was not a motivating factor for the BGU participants' enrollment. Hardworking and dedicated King High faculty were in short supply. Sadly, these individuals' efforts were typically overshadowed by the school's extensive and complicated history of subpar performance on a variety of measures.

According to Black Girls United members, King High School lived up to its poor academic reputation—which students generally attributed to the teaching faculty's wide-ranging character flaws. In various discussions with BGU learners, individuals branded King High educators as lazy and aloof. In fact, during the fourth Black Girls United meeting, a student named Rikesha remarked, "Too many teachers act like they don't wanna be here. They assign you work, and then they do they own thing, like we ain't even there! Like they don't have an important job to do!" (Rikesha, BGU class, Week 4). For 10 uninterrupted minutes, students dialed into their encounters with King High educators, and collectively painted an image of the urban public school teacher as discourteous, entitled, and slothful. Furthermore, participants declared that urban school practitioners believed that they benefitted "at risk" youth by simply showing up to work. One of my interviewees, Ashanti, was an eleventh-grader at the time of our Week 4 class discussion. After listening to Rikesha's remark, Ashanti took pleasure in demonstrating her math teacher, Mr. Abacha's particularly casual demeanor. Slumped in her chair with crossed arms, Ashanti shouted:

> Yep, cuz' [Mr. Abacha] don't care! Look, this what he do. [Pretending to be a male teacher, she deepens her voice] "Open up your book and turn to page 52. Read til' you get to the end of the chapter. Answer the questions at the end, and turn the work in by Friday." [Rising, and returning to her normal, seated position] If you give me the work on Monday, *why* is it due on Friday? Look,

don't give me that much time to do this *stupid little work*! That's just rude! (Ashanti, BGU class, Week 4)

In my interviews with a sub-sample of former BGU members, I sought to corroborate the sentiments above, which were expressed in video footage from over four years before this research study commenced. I was deeply disturbed by Black Girls United participants' descriptions of educators as individuals who assign bookwork, and subsequently, ignore students. Thus, I asked each of the seven former BGU learners to describe "typical experiences" with teachers back when they were in high school. A common theme across *each* interview was that the average teacher's disposition and pedagogical strategies made students feel unimportant and invisible—as if urban youth were not a worthy investment of their time. Tanya suggested that the behavior of those educators was foreseeable, since she and her peers were low-income people of color, attending an economically under-resourced school:

> I think teachers were way too comfortable because they were teaching kids who they thought didn't *"give a fuck"* about education. And the few of us who went home and complained to our parents ended up shut down. Because we just poor Black kids. And, you know, Latinos too. You know, we wasn't at Beverly Hills High. [King] students and parents didn't have the money or the power to get rid of those teachers. We wasn't rich White kids, so … like, we just had to deal with it. (Tanya, Interview #2, December 22, 2012)

When I asked Tanya to elaborate on her allegation that practitioners perceived she and her peers as individuals who devalued education, she suggested that youth can easily discern the difference between teachers who care authentically, and others, who *pretend* to care. Tanya noted that student disengagement is a consequence of the latter:

> I don't think [negligent teachers] were *really* invested in us in the first place. I think they automatically came in like, "These kids ain't about to amount to much." And you know, we could tell! So, you know, *all hell breaks loose* in the classroom! Like, that's why they couldn't control their classrooms. Ain't nobody about to listen to you! You can't keep students' attention if the teaching sucks *and* we know that you could care less about us! You act like you

don't care if I'm here or not. So, you may as well just pack up and go back home. [Laughing] Shoot, I may as well just go back home! (Tanya, Interview #2, December 22, 2012)

The notion that most educators enter into classrooms with the assumptions that urban students of color (a) don't want to learn, and (b) will lead trivial lives was consistent throughout the interviews. During my conversation with Kenya, she noted, "There were some teachers who didn't seem like they were there for our best interest to learn. *They* were smart. *They* went to college. But they didn't believe in *us*. So they weren't helping *us* get there. There wasn't any kind of motivation per se. They weren't pushing us to do better" (Kenya, Interview #2, January 12, 2013).

Overall, the Black Girls United participants agreed that numerous teachers at King High School were impediments to student success. Although individuals recognized that the overwhelming majority of their teachers had a firm grasp of their respective subject matter, and had achieved high levels of formal education— the learners maintained that uninspired and disenchanted practitioners were the mainspring of countless King High students' perpetual academic failure. Ashanti pointed out:

> The teachers were a barrier to student success. They didn't offer a helping hand. As a matter of fact, they were openly content with student failure. On a average day I'd hear a teacher say, "I don't gotta be here, *you do*. I don't need to graduate, *you do*. I'm getting paid one way or the other." So it kind of made me feel like, *what the fuck* am I really trying for? As long as I pass, I'm good. But I think most kids were turned off where they didn't even care about passin' Like, "I'm not about to try to go out my way and the teacher don't care." It's not like them teachers were really tryna' give me advice or sit me down, and really work with me. I honestly think the graduation rates would have been much higher if more teachers actually cared and realized that *we matter too*. (Ashanti, Interview #2, December 1, 2012)

Unmotivated teachers, who also carried deficit-ideologies about urban Black girls, amplified BGU students' feelings of obscurity—which youth simultaneously confronted in their communities. In the vignette that launched the discussion of *invisibility*, a student named Tanisha declared, "… we ain't *got shit*, cuz we *ain't shit!*" (BGU Class, Week 3). Although Tanisha's observation was blunt, it was also commendable, as she valiantly declared—in front of her peers and me—that society regarded Black women and girls as disposable. Tanisha's comment captured the sentiments expressed by other BGU youth across a four-year time lapse and myriad data sources. As Ashanti mentioned in the quote above, the individuals in Black Girls United wanted the world to know that they "matter too." Yet, further analysis of the data revealed a glaring spotlight that functioned as an unwelcomed instrument of social control and gender stratification, which was juxtaposed against learners' *invisibility*.

Hyper-Visibility

Ubiquitous messages of African American women's inferiority were an unremitting threat to the students in Black Girls United. Reductive representations of Black women and girls plastered across television and movie screens, and egregious acts of racialized sexist discourse were the norm in popular and hip-hop cultures. Historically, stereotypical images such as the loyal Mammy, the emasculating Sapphire, and the overtly sexual Jezebel have suppressed African American women and girls' opportunities to secure their recognition as human beings and invaluable contributors to the tapestry of U.S. society (Collins, 2000; Rose, 1994). Black Girls United participants identified three primary archetypes that functioned as cultural icons of African American femininity: the Black woman as anti-intellectual, "ghetto," and hypersexual. According to the participants in this study, these messages typically originated from the media and were perpetuated—whether out of malice or ignorance—by teachers and other students at King High School.

Danger: Educated Black Woman

One of the most marginalizing representations of Black women and girls that students encountered was the belief that African American women are unintelligent. The following field note illuminates a scenario in which a student named Latrice took the initiative to oppose the popular trope:

> Today, [Latrice] walked into our meeting wearing the most AWESOME shirt. On the front, in large, bold red lettering, it read "Smart Black Woman," and "SURPRISED?" in capital letters on the back. After I complemented [Latrice] on her shirt, I asked her to explain its meaning. She told me that she was wearing it "in case people are confused." She was specifically referring to her peers and some of her teachers at [King], who have made inaccurate assumptions about her intellectual potential, and the aptitude of Black girls in general. I'm most excited about the other reason behind her shirt. [Latrice's] manager at [Eternally Young] made a comment that she was "shocked" that [Latrice] was applying to such prestigious universities. Her manager assumed that she didn't have the grades for college—especially universities like USC and Loyola Marymount. [Latrice] explained that the scenario with her manager inspired her to have the t-shirt made. She's wearing it to work today. Simply brilliant! (Journal 1, Entry 12, p. 32)

Latrice was a twelfth-grade honors student at King High School. The decision to take on a part-time job stemmed from her desire to save money for college, and assist her mother and father with household expenses. Latrice's manager was oblivious to the degree to which her comment reinforced numerous other messages that Latrice had received regarding her perceived intellectual inferiority. At the time of the incident, Latrice's cumulative grade point average was a 3.9, and she was a highly competitive candidate for some of the nation's most esteemed post-secondary institutions. However, she often found herself insulted by the expectation that urban Black girls are incapable of attaining high levels of academic achievement.

During my interview with Nia, she shared a story similar to Latrice's. Nia was another exemplar of a young woman who did not fit the "dumb Black girl" mold. Nia recalled:

> When I went to [Pierson High] the way I spoke, it changed. Well, not changed. It was just different because I was with kids from different backgrounds. A lot of other races, you know? So when I came to [King], a lot of my teachers and other students were like, "You're so articulate." People would actually say that! "Oh, you're so smart. You speak so well." Like, I get that I didn't necessarily sound exactly the same as students at [King], but is that really a sign of

intelligence? Because I was smart before I enrolled at [Pierson], ok! But yeah, people at [King] would be like, "*Where are you from?*" And I'm like, "Um … down the street people!" (Nia, Interview #2, December 8, 2012)

Although Nia voiced her analysis four years after high school, as she reflected on her adolescence, I recognized that she and Latrice shared a similarly poignant sentiment. As high school students, both young women had refused to accept the widespread belief that African American girls were inherently unintelligent, and they engaged in various resistance strategies to combat threats to internally defined definitions of themselves.

In our fourth Black Girls United meeting, we discussed the African American tradition of utilizing education as a site of resistance. Students had previously read Chapter Nine of Patricia Hill Collins's *Black Feminist Thought: Knowledge, Consciousness, and the Politics of Power* (2000). The chapter entitled "Rethinking Black Women's Activism" illuminated how Black women acknowledged the "activist potential of education," and skillfully utilized their knowledge for self and community uplift (p. 210). An eleventh-grader named Ria led the conversation and developed a PowerPoint presentation that highlighted numerous famous (e.g., Oprah) and less known (e.g., Anna Julia Cooper) African American women who valued education as a cornerstone of Black community advancement. In the exchange that followed, the participants discussed the importance of sharing what they learned in the BGU meeting with their girl-identified peers, who were not members of BGU. The learners agreed that many young women have internalized—at least to some degree—the "Black girls are stupid" stereotype as a consequence of being bombarded with such misrepresentations. A ninth-grader named Erykah stated the following:

> Yeah, I'm gonna pass this along, because we need to stop dumbing ourselves down. It's a lot of girls here who think that being smart is whack. But you know, you can't just listen to everything you hear on TV because that's make believe. *Being stupid is not cute! People are going to just call you ghetto!* And I get that some girls might just want some attention— but it's like *why?* What's wrong with being a smart, educated Black woman? You don't have to be dumb to keep somebody's attention. (Erykah, BGU class, Week 4)

In numerous conversations with and among the participants of BGU, individuals acknowledged how society regarded African American women and girls as a population that held a variety of inferior traits. In the statement above, Erykah proclaimed that countless African American girl learners' perceived intellectual inferiority was typically associated with another contemporary stereotype: "the ghetto Black girl."

The Illusive Image of "the Ghetto Black Girl"

In my experience as a teacher at King High School, the term "ghetto" was by far the most commonly exercised slur against African American young women, and my interviews with former Black Girls United students revealed the rabid nature of its use both inside and outside of the school context. In the first round of interviews, my goal was for the young women to reflect on their perspectives of their personal and family histories, schooling experiences, and orientation towards school *prior* to joining Black Girls United. Moreover, I sought to determine individuals' understandings of the social and academic landscape of King High. For each interview, I asked participants to recall "How Black girls were perceived at [King] High." Five of the seven former BGU members included the term "ghetto" in their responses. As such, I requested that these students expand on their ideas and define the term. Their replies are below:

> Black girls were ghetto—meaning, they brought the drama. (Brittney, Interview #1, October 19, 2012)
>
> It was the typical stereotype—that she was going to end up on welfare with so many kids, and claiming, "Oh, I don't know who the child's father is." If you're ghetto, you're just classless. (Erykah, Interview #1, November 16, 2012)
>
> The expectation was for Black girls to be the stereotypical loud, ghetto girl who just has children all about and doesn't want to do something better for herself. Who's going to be stuck in the hood forever. (Kenya, Interview #1, November 9, 2012)
>
> Like, you're excessively loud regardless of where you're at. You use slang with everything, and you use hand gestures to get your point across. You

probably have multi-colored hair [laughing]. (Ashanti, Interview #1, October 5, 2012)

    If she's ghetto, she's loud, and not presentable. She wears long, ugly, distracting fingernails, and always chewing gum like she ain't never ate a meal. She's rowdy. She's hood. She's *not normal*. Doesn't do what normal people do. (Tanya, Interview #1, October 26, 2012)

The image of the "ghetto" Black girl first appeared in this chapter in the section on *invisibility*. Nia, who had participated in BGU during her eleventh and twelfth grade years, expressed disdain for individuals who called her ghetto—as the opprobrious epithet made her feel as if she were "nothing" (Interview #1, October 12, 2012). That is, voiceless, low-grade, and lacking purpose. The term ghetto reappears in this section on *hyper-visibility* because Black Girls United students identified the "ghetto Black girl" trope as one of the most seemingly impenetrable stereotypes about African American girl learners attending King High School. I searched across various data to decipher the ways in which BGU participants defined the expression. Collectively, students believed that the moniker was all-encompassing: girls identified as ghetto were considered dumb, unambitious, loud, low-income, and aggressive. Moreover, their behaviors were so uncouth that they exceeded the bounds of acceptability.

    It is critical to note that the former BGU participants agreed that the description mentioned above was a fitting portrayal of a *small minority* of Black girl adolescents at King High School. However, the interviewees also acknowledged that their definitions were tremendous overgeneralizations about the character of young Black women as a whole. Further, the Black Girls United members recalled how the insidious nature of representations of young Black women as ghetto consequently shaped King High teachers' interactions with these youth. During a BGU meeting, an eleventh-grader named Lisa described this phenomenon:

    I don't know what teachers think about Hispanic females, but they think that *we* are hopeless and have no future. So they treat a lot of students like future baby mama's and welfare recipients. No expectations. No standards. They act surprised if you get an answer right on a quiz. And you know who they think are the potential welfare queens? The loud girls who come in late and disrupt the class. Those are the ones who really get a bad rep, cuz teacher's think they just gon' be havin' babies and collectin' checks. After [Marquetta] came in late to period four, she sat down and started talking to the girl behind her. I heard [Ms. Jenkins] tell her—in front of the whole class—she was like, "[Marquetta] you should work on your posture and sit up straight. You gon' need a strong back when you're *barefoot and pregnant for the fourth time*, waiting on your check from the state!" I was like damn, when I come in late is that what she be thinkin' about me too? (Lisa, BGU class, Week 2)

According to Lisa, educators often assumed that Black girl learners who arrived late to class and engaged in teenage chatter would inevitably end up jobless, with multiple children whom they were incapable of supporting. In discussions with and among other BGU members, students recalled several examples of teacher's interactions with Black girls who did not fit the mold of Eurocentric femininity (i.e., passive, quiet, and obedient). Their conversations echoed Fordham's (1993) assertion that "loudness" is often damaging to Black girl adolescents' academic achievement. Practitioners traditionally characterize African American girls' heightened oral volume as a contrarian threat to the Eurocentric prescriptions of gender that are reinforced in schools. Moreover, the way in which a student's perceived "loudness" is intrinsically linked to her sexuality is an added attack on the character of African American girl learners.

Sexual Immorality

Low-income Black women and girls' alleged hyper-sexuality is a product of the mutually constructing systems of racism, classism, and sexism. Images of the "Bad Black Mother" and "Welfare Queen" date back to the 1960s, but gained increased popularity throughout the Reagan/ Bush era (Collins, 2000; Sears, 2010). During this time, the negative rhetoric and denigration of poor and working-class Black women severely limited social welfare support for these individuals who had been deemed lazy. The lingering image of the African American woman who takes advantage of public assistance and is unable to control her reproduction has remained consistent in contemporary discourse about urban Black girls (e.g., stigmas associated with teenage pregnancy). Many of the participants in Black Girls United were acutely aware of this externally defined construct of Black womanhood, and critiqued how it appeared in the social exchanges between young men and young women students at King High:

> Every year they created this ho list. It was basically a list of girls—usually Black girls—who supposedly slept around with a lot of dudes. Some of 'em already had babies. It was crazy because the list circulated around the whole school and it was embarrassing for the girls. And it was unfair because even if it wasn't true, the whole school was gonna think you were that way, regardless. And you were going to get teased and talked about for the rest of your years at [King]. So it was like, whatever you do, you better stay off that list. (Kenya, Interview #2, January 12, 2013)

The "Ho List," like the image of the Welfare Queen, was hazardous to African American girl students' perceived sexual morality at King High School. A young woman who was labeled promiscuous bore a proverbial scarlet letter on her chest, and was a victim of eternal shaming and public scrutiny. The irony here is that while King High youth berated certain Black girls for their purported sexual activity, the young women also received the message that selling their sexuality was a viable (and often praiseworthy) means of escaping poverty.

Television shows such as VH1's *The Flavor of Love* featured predominately Black and Latina women, who participated in various (habitually sexual) challenges to compete for the affection of rapper and celebrity, Flavor Flav. Several of the women on the show have since utilized their 15 minutes of fame as a platform for new endeavors in the entertainment industry. Likewise, the narrative of women exploiting their sexuality in exchange for an improvement in their economic and social status was also present in hip-hop music. For instance, in Lil' Wayne and Birdman's "Stuntin Like My Daddy," Wayne boasted, "When I was 16 I bought my first Mercedes Benz. I must've fucked a thousand bitches and they girlfriends." The theme of the materialistic, sexualized Black woman that was present in a multitude of popular music in the early 2000s was at the center of Karrine Steffans's infamous memoir, *Confessions of a Video Vixen* (2005). Pop culture critics heralded Steffans's novel as the harbinger of how-to-get-rich books for video vixens longing for financial independence and entrepreneurship.

Aside from providing fodder for water cooler conversations, these tremendously influential images taught young Black girls that if all else fails (or if school becomes too challenging), you could sell your sexuality in the name of social mobility. A tenth-grade student in our third Black Girls United meeting struggled with this notion:

> The only opportunities they make African American women seem like they can do is be video vixens. Like oh you're an African American woman, just go and be a video whore and that's how you're gonna succeed and become successful. It's like ... I don't know. It's weird. [Shifting into a softer, questioning tone] But, what are these girls supposed to do tho', if they didn't go to school or anything? Is it necessarily a bad thing to dance in videos? Long as [the men] aren't touching you and stuff, right? Like, what if that's all she can do to feed her family? I don't know. I guess—I guess it's not right for her to be dancing naked in front of all those men. *Especially if she likes it.* Man, I don't know. I guess I'm just confused. [Nervous laughter] (Kiera, BGU class, Week 3)

Some students in BGU affirmed the belief that it was acceptable to be overtly sexual to make ends meet—yet, the behavior was disdainful if carried out with the intent of personal pleasure. This principle remained a constant source of query and critique for the participants in this study. Together, perpetual [mis]representations of African American women and girls as anti-intellectual, ghetto, and overly sexual were the primary source of students' feelings of *hyper-visibility*. These controlling stereotypes functioned to obscure the true source of young Black women's subordination: the simultaneity of racial oppression, patriarchal tyranny, and the class stratification inherent to capitalist economic structure.

Outliers: Undercurrents of Love and Empowerment

In Venus Evans-Winters's (2011) ethnography, she examines the situational factors that aid low-income and working-class Black girls in developing resilient academic behaviors. In large part, multiple systems of support buoyed African American girl learners' educational persistence. The bi-directional and simultaneous positive influences

from family, community organizations, *and* school aided Black girl adolescents in negotiating the race, class, and gender stressors that they
encountered at school and in their neighborhoods. The participants in
Black Girls United similarly described a variety of influences—both
inside and outside of school—that inspired learners to continue their
educational pursuits in the face of the barriers previously discussed
(i.e., *invisibility* and *hyper-visibility*). Examples of such outliers are students' reports of the *protective mechanisms* employed by their parents
and guardians.

In my first interview with Lisa, she discussed the challenges of
attending high school as a foster care youth. From 2004 to 2008, King
High experienced an increase in the number of adolescents in out-of-
home care—or individuals who lived with relatives as opposed to traditional foster families. When Lisa was in the eleventh grade, her mother's
drug habit threatened she and her siblings' stability and well-being.
Like many other students at King High, Lisa was forced to find alternative housing with a family member—a time, which Lisa described as
highly volatile. In the years that followed, Lisa's aunt was her primary
caretaker, and the family resided in various neighborhoods across
South Los Angeles. In our first interview, Lisa described those communities as "jacked up and depressing," with the "usual drug addicts and
prostitutes" (Interview #1, November 2, 2012). Although the situation
was not ideal, Lisa's aunt worked several jobs to equip her with adequate material resources and academic supports. In our conversation,
Lisa noted:

> With my aunt, we lived in some apartments that were just a "step up" from
> the projects. A whole bunch of poor Black folks, and everybody on Section
> 8. And I didn't realize just how poor we were back then, but my aunt was
> struggling to pay her bills. But you know what, we was always taken care of.
> Like, we had decent clothes and new shoes when we needed them. And now
> when I think back, *it's like, wow!* She did that so we would think that we was
> just like everybody else. Because when I went to school, the kids with the
> money had on those same new [shoes]. So it was kind of like, my aunt, she did
> things that made it seem like we weren't struggling. Like, to look out for us.
> So I didn't really know that I was more poor than the next kid, even though
> we really, *really* were struggling sometimes. (Lisa, Interview #1, November
> 2, 2012)

Lisa's aunt worked vigorously and strategically to avoid the teasing and alienation that her niece would inevitably confront if she were stigmatized as "more poor" than her peers. In my analysis of the data sources, I encountered additional examples of parents' *protective mechanisms*. For instance, several parents and guardians made concerted efforts to limit their children's exposure to neighborhood gangs and potential bullying. In the following excerpt, Brittney describes how her mother drove her to school each morning as a *protective mechanism*, and eventually arranged for Brittney to obtain a vehicle during her senior year of high school.

> For me, I feel like I didn't have to worry about getting harassed by gangbangers like other kids when they had to walk to school, or when they came home from school. Because my parents made sure that no matter what, I wasn't going to be around that. *My mom, especially.* She used to give me rides to school all the time, and then when I was in the 11th grade she asked my granddad if he would buy me a car—cuz she and my dad knew they couldn't afford to get me one. My mom is close to her dad, and I'm like close to my granddad. If I didn't have my granddad, I wouldn't be driving around. He purchased my first car and my second. Cause he saw how I was doing in school. And they wanted to make sure that there weren't any distractions. And so, he bought my first car when I was fifteen and a half. (Brittney, Interview #1, October 19, 2012)

Several of the BGU members' parents and guardians were unswervingly determined to forge the best lives possible for their children. Brittney's mother and Lisa's aunt's *protective mechanisms* are two examples from a collection of many. These stories contradict the dominant narrative about the parents of urban students of color and the purported limited degree to which these individuals participate in the educational pursuits of their offspring (Lightfoot, 2004). Although most of the BGU participants' parents were unable to attend PTA meetings or chaperone field trips, they were motivating forces, who made personal sacrifices to promote their children's educational achievement. A student named Bianca substantiated this claim in a written reflection about her mother. Bianca recalled, "… and when I'm threatened by failure, I think of her commitment to my success. She pushes me to be my best. Don't nobody hold me down like my mama …" (Bianca, BGU Class, Week 5).

In addition to parents and guardians' *protective mechanisms* as inspiring outliers, BGU participants encountered *small serendipities* at King High School that challenged the largely disempowering nature of schooling for these youth. As mentioned in Chapter Three, 87 percent of the members of BGU (26/30 students) were enrolled in the Apprenticeship Magnet—the program in which I taught. In my examination of the data, I discovered that the Apprenticeship Magnet's custom of creating opportunities for students to experience the same teacher for multiple classes—was critical to BGU participants' ability to sustain themselves in an extremely challenging educational environment. Naturally, when a BGU learner encountered a "bad" teacher several years in a row, it adversely affected her enthusiasm towards school (as revealed earlier in the chapter). However, when youth cultivated meaningful relationships with authentically caring faculty, they flourished socially and academically. In my interview with Erykah, she proclaimed:

> I *love* Ms. Johnson! I had her for the 9th and 11th grade. Like, you could tell she *really* cared about her students. And having her for two years helped because she really pushed me to grow as a student and she's the reason why I joined the [Church Club] and the [Living for Literacy] program. She pushed all of us. She was just like, "You should really do it, [Erykah]," and I just joined because she said so. I trusted her because she had already taught me for two years, and you know—by then—she really knew me and knew my likes and dislikes. I wasn't even thinkin' about joining clubs or anything, but it really made me feel like a leader. *I felt limitless when I was around her.* Because she made me think outside the box and do something positive for myself. (Erykah, Interview #2, January 19, 2013)

As Erykah mentioned, teachers who embodied authentically caring dispositions regularly introduced students to extracurricular activities and encouraged youth to engage in various positive social and academic pursuits. In my conversations with BGU participants, the members revealed how they were impressed when—on a rare occasion—an educator pushed them to think outside of the box and pursue an endeavor that students had considered initially unattainable. In the quote above, Erykah stated that when she was in Ms. Johnson's presence, she felt "limitless"—which was a powerful space to occupy, even if transitorily. A noteworthy finding that emerged from the data is the number of African American women, of all ages, were highlighted as "inspiring" educators. In my interviews with former BGU members, several participants spoke candidly about how they developed a coincidental closeness with Black women faculty at King High. Because I taught four of the seven interviewees, BGU youth frequently included me in the group of African American women role models. In my interview with Ashanti (Interview #2, December 1, 2012), she jokingly recounted how our relationship had evolved from my demand that she come to class on time:

Interviewer: Ok, so tell me, how did our relationship develop?

Ashanti: [Laughing] I was comin' late to summer school for like three days in a row, and you said, "Hey if you don't come on time you ain't passin." What you need me to do to help you?' So right there I was like, "*Oh, she one of them teachers that give a fuck.*"

Interviewer: And so, you automatically started coming on time after that? It was that easy?

Ashanti: [Laughing] Hell naw! I remember you pulling me to the side like, you was like, "Let me tell you something. You don't show up on time to my class, you gon' fail." And like the first day I thought you were just, like, bullshitting. I was just like yeah alright. And I think like the next day you was like, "How can I help you? Tell me how I can help you." And I was just like what you mean? And you was like, "I can call you in the morning. You need to get woke up?" And I was just like yeah, I guess. So I gave you my phone number. I remember it was on a Friday cause I was like this lady ain't gon' call and wake me up, she gon' forget. And I remember that Monday morning you called at like 5 o'clock in the morning. *I was pissed* when my phone was going, I'm like *what*?! I'm like *she really called my phone*, like *she really called my phone and woke me up*! And it was like after that, everyday you called and woke me up and I was on time. *Every single day* after that I was on time. Fo' real. I used to dread it in the morning! I used to know you was gon' call, too. Sometimes I just wanted to cut my phone off, but I'd be like *I gotta go to school, I gotta go to school.*

Interviewer: [Laughing] *What*?! You were going to cut off your phone on me?! So tell me, why'd you keep it on if you knew that call was coming?

Ashanti: Like shit, I don't even know! It was like, I knew you'd be disap-
            pointed. And it got my attention, like *why the fuck do she care?*
            You took the time out of your busy mornin' to call me. Like, it
            kind of made me open my eyes a little more or kind of push
            me. Made me want to do better. So you kept callin' and I kept
            answerin' and that's how we got close.

Ashanti's mother typically left for work a few hours before it was time for her to get dressed for school. Without an adult in the home to hold Ashanti accountable for waking up on time, she would often oversleep, and arrive at school a half hour late. Before enrolling in my summer school course, Ashanti was able to pass her classes with a C or better because—according to her—former teachers were not "big on attendance." My expectation for Ashanti to arrive to class on time, and my efforts to provide a wake-up call each morning, were confirmation of my genuinely caring disposition and my desire for Ashanti to reach her full academic potential. Because she had not experienced such high expectations from previous teachers, when I challenged Ashanti to simply try harder, it "opened" her eyes, and influenced her to strive towards excellence in my class.

Additionally, a handful of other African American women faculty mentioned by students also performed caring in ways that were sincere and heartfelt. In keeping with the tradition of Black womanist educators, the "care" described by the participants integrated unrelenting displays of personal responsibility and an obligation for collective advancement (Roseboro & Ross, 2009). These teachers characteristically went above and beyond the call of duty (i.e., providing rides to school, making home visits, and feeding students), and were often labeled as pushy *and* loving. Another Black Girls United student named Tanisha asserted that these Black women educators stayed "on yo' head"— meaning they frequently questioned students' whereabouts, monitored individuals' academic progress, and confronted youth who engaged in harmful social behaviors—thereby embodying a "no nonsense" motherly affection.

Together, the *protective mechanisms* employed by the parents and guardians of BGU participants, and the *small serendipities* at King High School served as inspiring outliers that re-invigorated students amidst unfavorable community and school conditions. Notwithstanding the positive influences of these outliers, African American girl students' *persistent* isolation and "race-gender differentiated socialization" significantly threatened youth's self-esteem and perceptions of self-worth. This, in turn, resulted in learners' application of oppositional behaviors to preserve their humanity in the face of abundant injustices (Grant, 1984, p. 98).

Conclusion: Resistance Against Multiple Adversities

The students in Black Girls United faced innumerable challenges both in and out of school that jeopardized the development of their fragile identities and sparked feelings of *invisibility* and *hyper-visibility*. In general, the learners articulated two unique methods of negotiating these barriers. On some occasions, youth participated in what Robinson and Ward (1991) refer to as *resistance for liberation*, wherein students' attitudes and behaviors countered normative discourse about Black women and girls, and typically resulted in self and community elevation. Conversely, there were circumstances in which students engaged in resistance strategies such as ditching school or mouthing off to keep from being silenced. These survival techniques were recurrent and self-defeating for many Black Girls United participants. Overall, I identified a variety of oppositional behaviors and a strong undercurrent of resilience in each participant.

Resistance for Liberation's Sake

One redemptive resistance tool that students regularly utilized was deliberately working against the stereotype that African American young women are intellectually inferior. Although the participants in BGU represented a broad spectrum of academic performance (most students held B and C averages), some individuals had aspirations of attending prestigious universities, developing a stable career path, and giving back to their communities. To meet their goals and transcend systemic barriers, BGU participants often called upon the strength of close family members and highly regarded African Americans in the diaspora. In a field note that I composed after our fourth Black Girls United meeting, I described my initial perceptions of students' pursuits of excellence:

> Today we talked about goals. Long-term goals and short-term goals. I was in the presence of future rock stars: professional dancers, lawyers, surgeons, business owners, and teachers. I am encouraged by their vision. Who do they look to for inspiration? They call on their mama's, older siblings, and elders. And of course, there's always Oprah. (Journal 2, Entry 5, p. 14)

Although BGU members' grades did not consistently reflect their post-graduation ambitions, the participants valued a strong work ethic and a clever mind—an outlook that is common in Black working-class communities. Some Black Girls United youth were taught the adage "lifting as we climb" at a young age, and understood that collective responsibility was at the root of any successful Black person's journey. Erykah's upbringing was indicative of the spirit of determination and community uplift that many BGU learners personified. In our first interview she stated:

> When I was little my mother used to tell me, "You gonna be somebody. I want my kids to do better than me." Because as Black women, you know, people think we're probably not gonna do well. We're going to be looked down on regardless. And so, I have to be on top of it, cause if I fail I'm making everyone in the race look bad. And that's how it is for Black people 'cause if you think about it, you watch the news, a robbery happens. I used to always catch myself, I'd be like "Dang, why does he gotta be black?" [Laughing] It hurts to see my own people embarrass themselves, especially after what all of our people went through. But I felt like, I can use my education and street smarts to get success. So I used that as my advantage. It's like, okay I may go to [King], but I'ma get my education, *I'ma' get mines regardless*. And it was important to help my peers to. I used to have friends, they would be like "Oh well this teacher doesn't even care, so why am I even doing this work?" And I would find myself, like, being the mama of the group, encouraging everyone like, "You're doing this for yourself, and for your family and community. Don't give them the satisfaction of failing, cause then all along they're gonna be like, "Yes I was right. That student doesn't have the potential of being anything." (Erykah, Interview #1, November 16, 2012)

Surpassing society's low expectations for African American women and girls was a chief objective for students in Black Girls United. As Erykah mentioned, individuals worked towards academic success and acknowledgment of their intellectual aptitude—with the intention of uplifting one's relatives, community members, and other Black people in the process.

Likewise, there were several other BGU participants whose priorities centered on undermining an equally prominent image of Black womanhood: the sexually irresponsible, poor Black woman. These youth were not necessarily interested in attending the nation's most prestigious universities; however, they similarly engaged in liberatory acts of resistance. For a handful of Black Girls United members, graduating from high school and avoiding teenage pregnancy loitered at the forefront of their desires. Although several of these youth were not sexually active when they joined the organization, King High students' declining graduation rates and the negative portrayal of Black single mothers in the media inspired students to be the first in their families to earn a high school diploma and many individuals vowed to meet this goal before embarking on motherhood. The following list includes the short-term and long-term goals of a BGU student named Patrice and reveals her desire to complete her education before starting a family (Patrice, BGU class, Week 4):

1. Graduate high school → Make parents proud, 1st generation
2. Get my AA Degree in communications → Get a good job
3. Get married to a fine Black man → No kids
4. Start a family → 3 kids

Patrice was in the eleventh grade when the members of Black Girls United listed their academic, career, and personal goals. Her top priority was to make her parents proud and become the first person in her family to earn a college degree. Although she longed for marriage and children, developing oneself personally and intellectually before starting a family was Patrice's priority—which echoed numerous BGU learners' sentiments. Kenya, like Patrice, imagined becoming the first in her family to graduate high school and eventually matriculate to college. In her list, she explained that her mother dropped out of high school in the tenth grade, and her sister became pregnant at 15 and never obtained the credits required to graduate. Thus, it was critical for Kenya to "do something better" with her life, "instead of what they did or what society [tells Black girls] to do" (Kenya, BGU Class, Week 4). Although a vast majority of Black Girls United youth sought to disrupt oppressive stereotypes about African American women and girls, there were undoubtedly moments wherein individuals engaged in counter-productive behaviors.

Just Tryin' to Get By

Each member of Black Girls United had aspirations of graduating high school, which was an indubitable expectation. However, the uninspiring conditions for learning at King High School created abundant obstacles for students to attain the success they envisioned. One tremendous barrier for participants was maintaining high grade point averages. Remaining motivated while attending classes with disenchanted teachers and lackluster curricula proved to be a challenging feat for BGU youth. As such, learners frequently conveyed demeanors that threatened their ability to pass their classes and graduate on time.

Sadly, a BGU participant named Daniella—who was a senior during the first year of the program—struggled to maintain a leg up in a course that was a prerequisite for college. As an AP (Advanced Placement) English student, Daniella was cognizant of her English teacher's low expectations and inability (or refusal) to create a captivating curriculum. The teacher, Mrs. [Ramirez], typically assigned work from the textbook that was uninteresting and easy to complete, relative to other AP-level courses that Daniella had formerly encountered. As a result, the students in Mrs. Ramirez' class would disengage by arriving late, listening to music during instructional time, and playing card games instead of completing the assignments. As a budding poet, Daniella utilized her time in Mrs. Ramirez' class to fine-tune her talents and created a book of poetry in lieu of completing the designated reading. As a result, Daniella failed the class in the first semester, having earned 32 percent of the total points. One day after school, Daniella shared a poem with me, which she had developed while Mrs. Ramirez read a newspaper at her desk. Teeming with enthusiasm, Daniella stood tall and recited the following:

> I am POOR
> Do you hear me?
> I am buried beneath your riches and your gold
> The weight of your wealth conceals my sound
> I am BLACK
> Do you see me?
> Racism dulls my radiance.
> With each slay of your whip, I fall deeper into an abyss of darkness.
> I am WOMAN
> Can you hear my cry?
> It lies deep within my womb. I am careful not to plea too loudly.
> For, I might awaken you.
> (Daniella, BGU student, Week 4)

After sharing her poem, Daniella insisted that I keep it. I tucked the crumpled sheet of paper away in the center of my second BGU journal, and I savored Daniella's brilliance for over four years. When I came across her writing during the data analysis phase, I was triggered by the tremendous impact that feelings of *invisibility* had on the African American girl adolescents in BGU. When I asked Daniella what prompted her to write that specific poem, she replied, "[Ms. Ramirez] could care less if I pass her class. Half the time, I don't think she even know I'm there. If she don't care, why should I?" (Journal 2, Entry 11, p. 20).

There was an enormous price to pay for feeling *invisible* at King High School. In my interview with Ashanti, she shared how her boredom with certain classes resulted in habitual ditching. As a consequence, she was only motivated to maintain a C average, which was the requirement for playing on the basketball team. After injuring her knee in the eleventh grade, though, Ashanti's was startled by the meager post-graduation options available to someone who did not have the grade point average required to attend a four-year university. Ashanti explained:

> Listen, I was just tryna' get by, that's what it really was. Making sure I had a C average, just to be able to play on the basketball team. *Cuz school was so damn boring*, like, I hated most of my classes. I really wanted to go to college after, get a Bachelor's degree, like try to get a scholarship and go to college. But, when I got hurt, all that changed. I had to get surgery 11th grade, and that messed up my last year of ball. But by then it was already too late. I couldn't go to no university cuz I was able to fail a lot of my classes and keep a overall C average and still play. I had D's in, like, the important classes for college, you know? Like if I put as much time as I put in basketball into school, *shit*, I would've been a straight A student. But that was hard to do at [King] cuz, like, what's the motivation? I ain't finna sit in no class if the teacher ain't teachin shit. But lookin back, I was a *student athlete*, not just a athlete. I should've been doing work in my classes regardless of them teachers. But you know, I was a kid. Needed inspiration or sumthin'. Dumb. And in the long run it fucks you. *Literally*. [Laughing] (Interview #1, October 5, 2012)

From the participants' perspectives, several of the Black Girls United members sacrificed their academic achievement, school engagement, and future life prospects to engage in behaviors that would conceivably inoculate youth from their distressing schooling environment. As Ashanti mentioned, urban adolescents needed to be "inspired" to attain academic success amidst severe educational inequities. For numerous young Black women participants in this study, cheerleading and athletics did not require students to maintain passing grades in the classes required for most colleges, which severely limited their options to pursue higher education in a competitive (i.e., university) setting. On the other hand, the individuals who managed to earn high grade point averages were alienated by the *invisibility* and *hyper-visibility* at King High, which impeded their evolving self-worth, and negatively impacted students' outlook on school. In the following, Nia described how the lack of stimulating programs for Black girl learners steered her into a perpetual state of longing:

> We were the lost generation. I really felt like they expected the Black girls at our school to be ok. They felt like, "We don't have to worry about the Black

girls." They can do all the gang intervention and all the male intervention. And they can bring in males from other places to come in and help with the boys. And there was nothing for the girls to do. Because it was like, "The girls are gonna make it." You know, they felt like they don't have to worry about us. The *Black* girls. They don't have to make any special programs for us. We can either cheerlead, play softball, run track, and *that's it*! (Nia, personal communication, October 3, 2011)

Before joining the organization, the participants in Black Girls United had desperately searched for an alternative space that affirmed their unique cultural backgrounds and intellectual capacities. In the reflection above, Nia craved a "special program" for Black girls that would encourage self-determination that manifested resistance to their shared group oppression. This sentiment, moreover, drew many young people to BGU. Ostensibly, there was "nothing to lose," and the lure of "something different" was appealing to several learners (Kenya, Interview #1, November 9, 2012). Members' yearning for more was unmistakable—and young Black women at King High, it seems, were hard-wired for resistance. It was under these conditions that a group of girls ventured into new territory, where they would journey together in sisterhood, solidarity, and audacious self-love.

Questions for Deeper Engagement

1. Black girls are a complex group who negotiate rich and varied interactions with educational institutions and in their communities. In what ways are these students *invisible* and *hyper-visible* in your particular educational community?
2. It is critical for Black girl learners to develop internally defined definitions of themselves in educational spaces, which challenges race-gender schemas that devalue Black femininity. Analyze the extra-curricular landscape of your institution. What opportunities are available for young Black women to construct resistance strategies against the barriers that they encounter within and beyond the schoolhouse? How, if at all, do you contribute to the growth and sustainment of these alternative spaces?

Notes

1 Tupac Shakur was a popular American rapper, who passed away in 1991 and rose
   to great prominence in 1994. In the field note above, I reference his 1993 hit song,
   "Keep Ya Head Up." Shakur originally dedicated the song to Latasha Harlins, a 15-
   year-old African-American girl, who was shot and killed in 1991 by Korean store
   owner, Soon Ja Du. Harlins's murder gained national attention when her perpetra-
   tor was merely fined, sentenced to probation, and required to complete community
   service as a consequence of his crime.
2 The phrase "a hard knock life" was originally a song title from the 1977 Broadway
   musical production, *Annie*. The upbeat tune makes light of an orphan girl's repeated
   and extreme misfortune during her residency in a children's group home. The jin-
   gle re-emerged in 1999 as a single from rapper Jay-Z's third album, Vol. 2 … Hard
   Knock Life. The context of the song was altered in Jay-Z's version, which highlights
   the social and economic trials of urban, inner city youth. As a result of the sustained
   popularity and global commercial success of Jay-Z's rap song, the phrase "a hard
   knock life" has become an anthem for adolescents in under-resourced communities
   across the nation.

References

Collins, P. H. (2000). *Black feminist thought: Knowledge, consciousness, and the politics of
    empowerment* (2nd ed.). New York, NY: Routledge.
Davis, A. Y. (1983). *Women, race & class*. New York, NY: Vintage Books.
Evans-Winters, V. E. (2005). *Teaching Black girls: Resiliency in urban classrooms*. New York,
    NY: Peter Lang.
Fordham, S. (1993). "Those loud Black girls": (Black) women, silence, and gender "pass-
    ing" in the academy. *Anthropology and Education Quarterly, 24*(1), 3–32.
Grant, L. (1984). Black females "place" in desegregated classrooms. *Sociology of
    Education, 57,* 98 111.
Harris-Perry, M. (2011). *Sister citizen: Shame, stereotypes, and Black women in America.*
    New Haven: Yale University Press.
hooks, b. (1984). *Feminist theory from margin to center*. Boston, MA: South End Press.
Lightfoot, D. (2004). "Some parents just don't care": Decoding the meanings of parental
    involvement in urban schools. *Urban Education, 39*(1), 91–107.
Morgan, J. (1999). *When chickenheads come home to roost: My life as a hip hop feminist.*
    New York, NY: Simon & Schuster.
Muhammad, C. G., & Dixson, A. D. (2008). Black females in high school: A statistical
    educational profile. *The Negro Educational Review, 59*(3–4), 163–180.

Robinson, T., & Ward, N. L. (1991). In C. Gilligan, A. G. Rogers, & D. L. Tolman (Eds.), *Women, girls & psychotherapy: Reframing resistance* (pp. 87–104). Binghamton, NY: The Haworth Press.

Rose, T. (1994). *Black noise: Rap music and Black culture in contemporary America.* Middletown: Wesleyan University Press.

Roseboro, D. L., & Ross, S. N. (2009). Care-sickness: Black women educators, care theory, and a hermeneutic of suspicion. *Educational Foundations, 23*(3/4), 19–40.

Sears, S. D. (2010). *The negotiation of power and identity within the Girls Empowerment Projects.* Albany: SUNY Press.

Smith, T. (2002). What happens when your hood is the last stop on the White flight express. In D. Hernandez & B. Rehman (Eds.), *Colonize this!: Young women of color on today's feminism.* Emeryville, CA: Seal Press.

Steffans, K. (2005). *Confessions of a video vixen.* New York: Harper Collins.

"My job is to somehow make them curious enough or persuade them, by hook or crook, to get more aware of themselves and where they came from and what they are into and what is already there, and just to bring it out. This is what compels me to compel them and I will do it by whatever means necessary."

~Nina Simone

Chapter Five

Unpacking the Pedagogy

In *Beyond The Methods Fetish: Toward a Humanizing Pedagogy*, Lilia Bartolomé calls for educators to abandon mechanistic applications of popular teaching strategies for racially, culturally, and linguistically subordinated student populations, and instead utilize a socio-historical approach to developing humanizing pedagogies for these learners (Bartolomé, 1994). In the previous chapter, I illuminated how Black girl youth's socio-political location sparked perpetual feelings of *invisibility* and *hyper-visibility* at King High School, which commonly stemmed from reductive and unimaginative curricular approaches. Additionally, I examined how this noisy and callous marginalization had harmful effects on students' orientation towards school. As an equity-minded Black woman educator and former King High student, I responded viscerally to these adolescents' marked alienation. I clung precariously to the idea that I could—with the support and guidance of my African American girl students—create a safe space that would arouse learners' intellectual power and potential, as well as support Black girls in cultivating viable resistance strategies against myriad oppressive forces.

As previous chapters have illuminated *why* I created Black Girls United, this chapter offers a glimpse into *how* the program functioned. In developing the structure of BGU, I invoked the scholarship of Black women practitioners—such as bell hooks, Gloria Joseph, and others who openly position their teaching practice within a Black feminist or womanist politic. Inspired by the philosophy "lifting as we climb,"[1] these luminaires employ a variety of instructional techniques that reflect their appreciation for education as an instrument for social mobility *and* a means of personal and community empowerment. Thus, my conceptualization of Black feminist pedagogy involved developing a framework that was inspired by these scholars—yet we also responded to the sensibilities of my unique group of urban, African American girl learners. Moreover, it is critical to acknowledge how my experiences as an African American woman in a particular time, location, and social context also informed the Black feminist pedagogical framework that I elucidate in the following sections.

Four key features were at the core of my teaching praxis in Black Girls United: *critical feminist literature, positioning students as change agents, a politicized ethic of care,* and *collectivity.* Each of these elements emerged naturally from my Black feminist practitioner standpoint, and I applied the four components simultaneously. However, it is important to note that the Black Girls United members' interpretations of their experiences in the program—which I obtained via individual interviews and other data sources (e.g., 35 hours of video recordings from BGU classes; my Black feminist curriculum; two years of field notes from in-class and out-of-class interactions; and student artifacts)—provided extensive insight into my re-articulation and utility of Black feminist pedagogy. In the sections that follow, I paint a vivid picture of the instructional landscape of BGU, and my efforts to take an "informed approach" to "potentially offset the unequal relations and discriminatory structures and practices" that young Black women at King High School endured both inside and outside of the classroom (Bartolomé, 1994, p. 412).

Critical Feminist Literature

Interviewer: Do you even remember doing the readings in [Black Girls United]? Because I know that obviously for the week that people had to lead, that person definitely had to do the reading to know what the heck we were talking about. But how do you think the readings played into the space? Could we have just eliminated the literature and had the same effect? You can be as honest as—

Brittney: [Interrupting] No! I think having—like the literature is a good part of it. It was important. And I always read. Cause if you don't have some opinions that offers perspectives, you don't know where to start. I mean you probably have a starting ground, but having something that's already written, that you can refer to and reflect on, is good. 'Cause it drives so much of the conversation. Which we needed, because *we were up there teaching, not you!* [Laughing] So the readings gave us something to compare our own experiences to. And that's what got us going.

In my interview with Brittney (Interview #2, December 15, 2012), she recounted how critical feminist literature was at the core of Black Girls United and served as the basis for our weekly discussions. In the planning stages of the organization, I kept a journal where I recorded my ideas. In that journal, I assembled a list of conversation topics based on exchanges with several of my students, as well as my understanding of their diverse struggles. Ultimately, the literature that I selected for the program emerged out of my list of potential foci. Some of the themes included: rectifying body image issues; demystifying intimate partner abuse; the hyper-sexualization of Black women in youth popular culture; money management and financial literacy; and setting long-term and short-term goals. To gather writing that reflected learners' social realities and cultural interests, I accumulated scholarship from various sources—including my home library. I also borrowed texts from friends and colleagues who graciously passed along relevant reading materials.

The Black Girls United curricula primarily included texts of resistance and contestation, which were authored by Black women and other women of color, and challenged conventional representations of non-White women in popular literature and the dominant media. I was hopeful that the material would spark members' attention, whether they agreed or disagreed with the writers' nuanced perspectives. I also intended to select weekly readings that triggered emotional and scholarly reactions from the participants. Because BGU was not a required course in which students would receive a grade,[2] it was critical that the literature was sufficiently engaging to sustain members' investment in the program and their intense desire to read each week.

Taking into consideration learners' wide-ranging grade and skill levels, I introduced the members to an assortment of texts (i.e., narrative literature, expository writing, and poetry). BGU participants drew on Joan Morgan's *When Chickenheads Come Home to Roost: My Life as a Hip Hop Feminist* (1999) as a starting ground for critiquing the misogyny in the rap lyrics of songs such as Too Short's (2003) "Shake That Monkey" (BGU class, Week 12). Additionally, in Stella Luna's (2002) *HIV and Me: The Chicana Version* the participants read about the shame that women of color HIV survivors endure (BGU class, Week 40). Moreover, *The Black Beauty Myth* by Sirena J. Riley (2002) served as an appealing starting point by which individuals could critique societal pressures to conform to Eurocentric standards of beauty (BGU class, Week 22).

As Brittney mentioned in the opening transcript, feminist literature drove our *student-led* conversations in Black Girls United. Each week, a member (or team of two learners) facilitated the discussion, and I rarely intervened—typically, to pose a question or offer a new viewpoint. Patricia Hill Collins (2000) reminds us that a distinguishing feature of a *safe space* is that it is free from the "surveillance of more powerful groups" (p. 111). As I fashioned the pedagogy of Black Girls United, I believed that it was imperative for the participants to have an opportunity to engage in critical dialogue that was self-orchestrated (i.e., students controlled the planning and facilitation of the lessons). While I was aware that as a teacher my presence alone might have intimidated some members, requiring the young women to lead our discussions was my attempt at limiting the potential threat of my positionality.

BGU facilitators generally followed the Socratic Seminar method of instruction. Presenters challenged their peers to think critically by engaging learners in a series of open-ended questions—to encourage exploration and divergent thinking over simply locating the "right" answer. When individuals struggled to produce critical questions for discussion, they asked for my assistance, and we co-constructed thought-provoking lessons. Furthermore, we solidified the weekly topics in advance, which provided the facilitator(s) with sufficient time to design interesting activities. In my second interview with Tanya, she explained how the organization of the program was central to its operation. She noted:

> [Our classes] were very organized. That was super important. We did lots of planning. But we always planned in advance. Like even when we went off topic in the [BGU] meeting and some member brought up, "Oh so next week we should talk about this," and we all agreed on it, then from that very moment it was a planning stage of well, "What's going to be stated? What are we gonna focus on? Do we want them to take something extra home with them to read and think about? Is it gonna be a Q&A? Or is it gonna be everyone starts discussion as whole?" And we would kind of base it around what we knew the members of [BGU] wanted to see or wanted to hear, or what intrigued them you know. (Tanya, Interview #2, December 22, 2012)

Tanya was the Vice President of BGU in the second year of the program, and she played a significant role in assisting the facilitators with developing the weekly lessons. Because there was a syllabus in place, most members planned their presentations two-to-three weeks in advance. However, there were some occasions in which the class spontaneously decided to examine an issue that was not included in the syllabus. In those instances, the student leaders had one week to prepare a lesson and distribute the required readings. The elected officials were responsible for ensuring that BGU participants remembered to attend each meeting and read the assigned literature. As such, student officers created reminder slips that were delivered to each member in their third- and fourth-period classes a day or two before our meetings. Often, handouts of the assigned reading accompanied the reminder slips.

Generally, our discussions commenced with a facilitator referencing a passage from a text. However, as Tanya mentioned in the quote above, the members of BGU worked diligently to locate exciting ways to spark dialogue. Sometimes, the presenter would open with an unsettling statement that was pertinent to the weekly theme, such as when Lisa aroused members' interest with the declaration that "Black women are unattractive" (Lisa, BGU class, Week 22). Typically, an assertion such as Lisa's generated numerous passionate responses from the learners. On other occasions, the facilitator would introduce the topic via a multimedia demonstration (e.g., PowerPoint presentations, video clips, or musical selections).

In my interviews with former BGU participants, individuals revealed that our meetings operated like college classes. The members believed that the critical feminist literature was rigorous, and each member was expected to come to class prepared, and ready to engage with her peers. As a former English teacher, I was aware that my high school students frequently skipped the assigned reading. Accordingly, when past BGU participants confirmed that they completed the majority of the texts— I was overwhelmed with disbelief. During the interviews, students attributed their willingness to read to three major characteristics of the feminist literature. In Black Girls United—unlike traditional classes— *each* text was relevant, current, and triggered an emotional response.

Attending a class that offered a multitude of *relevant* material was new to the students in BGU. Most learners claimed that the curriculum in their conventional classes failed to address real-life issues. For instance, in our eleventh Black Girls United meeting, Nia proclaimed that she valued the readings in the program because they were "original pieces" written by "real women" who spoke about "real issues" (Nia, BGU class, Week 11). In the following quote from Denise—extracted from a statement that she made during class in her second year of the program—she discussed how her disengagement from many of her high school classes was due to her disinterest in curriculum that was detached from her everyday life experiences:

> I feel like we don't get real world preparation in high school outside of [BGU].
> Like how we talk about how to conduct ourselves in a interview, or how to

get a good credit score. You know, where's the real life preparation? Even
with just how to *deal with people* in everyday life. Like, they don't teach us
that in school. But we expected to get good grades tho'. Even in spite of what
you're going through outside [of school]. But there isn't any, like *teaching*, you
know, to help us grow. (Denise, BGU class, Week 32)

From Denise's perspective, the typical high school program did not
assist students in navigating their personal lives or professional
endeavors. As an unintended consequence of Denise's disconnection
in many of her classes, she often ditched school and eluded a number
of important opportunities to learn. During our BGU meeting, Denise
explained why reading Cheryl Broussard's informative text, *The Black
Woman's Guide to Financial Independence* (1996)—which taught students
how to create a budget and decipher a credit score—were vital to her as
a high school senior. She noted that although those materials were not
"typical readings," they were integral to assisting her in "becoming a
responsible adult" (Denise, BGU class, Week 32).

According to the learners, another essential feature of the feminist
literature in Black Girls United is that it was relevant, *and* current—
which was not always the case in my traditional English classes. Like
most educators working in the *No Child Left Behind* climate of high-
stakes testing, I was desperately concerned with acquainting my
English students with a wide array of canonical texts, because they
were regularly present in the annual state exams. Consequently, my
ninth- and eleventh-grade English students did not *always* engage with
literature written in the twenty-first century. Although I had made a
concerted effort to introduce texts with culturally (including racially,
linguistically, and ideologically) relevant themes, the material was not
always contemporary. In the following statement from my interview
with Ashanti, she compared her frequent *disconnection* from the texts
in my eleventh-grade honors English class to her consistent *engagement*
with the literature in Black Girls United:

[In typical English classes] you gotta get through shit. You gotta learn stuff
like *A Raisin in the Sun*, and what's that book like nobody really gave a damn
about? [Recalling the text] Oh yeah, *Fences*! Now the whole storyline of it,
that's kind of like, *deep*. Like, I get it or whatever. But they was *boring as hell*

cuz' that was like *way* back in the day. But, in [BGU] we was always talkin'
about something we live around and what we was *really* going through as
teenagers. Stuff that will really catch like the teenager's eyes, and really get
them into it. So you know, it was a lot more interestin' to do those readings.
You can't sit and talk about like, something like *Fences* and expect us to relate.
(Ashanti, Interview #2, December 1, 2012)

Although both *A Raisin in the Sun* (1958) by Lorraine Hansberry and
August Wilson's *Fences* (1986) have garnered national recognition and
reverence as classic fictional plays, by Ashanti's teenage standards, both
texts were outdated, and therefore, inevitably unexciting. On the opposite end of the spectrum, according to the young women, the material
in Black Girls United was stimulating because we habitually examined
topics that were relevant to the lives of urban, African American female-
identified *teenagers*. For instance, we spent three consecutive weeks (i.e.,
three meetings) investigating why some of the young women at King
High School were participating in a movement to reclaim the term
"bitch" (BGU class, Weeks 13–15) through a textual analysis of Joan
Morgan's *When Chickenheads Come Home to Roost* (1999).

Working to dismantle patriarchy by reclaiming sexist epithets was
considered a hot topic—and in Black Girls United, we had the freedom
to explore the issue until the students were ready to move on. Although
the readings in my honors English class centralized and normalized
the ideas and sensibilities of people of color, we focused on topics that
were not necessarily intriguing for Black girl *adolescents*. Occasionally,
we covered young adult literature; however, I felt pressured to complete those texts quickly. To comply with the California Department
of Education's proposed pacing plan for satisfying the state standards
in English Language Arts, it was mandatory to stay on track with my
timeline.

The third and final feature of the feminist literature in Black Girls
United was the emotional reaction that most texts elicited from the
members. This revelation was possibly most evident during a class in
which several members shared personal accounts of sexual harassment
(BGU class, Week 36). Before our meeting, the learners read *How Sexual
Harassment Slaughtered, Then Saved Me* by Kiini Ibura Salaam (2002).
After approximately 20 minutes of dialogue, the participants were still

highly animated and enthusiastic about our discussion. When the bell rang to signal the end of lunch, numerous students booed with irritation and disappointment at the thought of having to return to their regular classes. After school, I wrote about the experience:

> *Amped. That's how I'm feeling today. The girls were so pissed when the bell rang for 5ᵗʰ period, that three students [jokingly] threatened to lock themselves in my classroom in protest. [Kiini Ibura] Salaam's reading had them on edge! Folks debated the difference between a woman and a lady, and if females who carried themselves as "unladylike" somehow incited sexual misconduct. The conversation was* heated! *There were smiles, hugs, and laughter. On the flipside there was anger, alienation, and indecision. And I LOVED EVERY MOMENT!* (Journal 3, Entry 19, p. 112)

The Black Girls United meetings were engrossing because we fearlessly examined subjects that were considered touchy (i.e., using the racial epithet *nigger* in friendly conversations, BGU class, Week 14), emotional (i.e., the skin color hierarchy in the African American community; BGU class, Week 22), or taboo even (e.g., girls and adolescents' genital mutilation; BGU class, Week 62). The passion that the literature triggered was an element of the program that former Black Girls United students vividly recalled, even years later. During my interview with Tanya, she explained that in BGU "there were *feelings* attached to the content. It wasn't like most classes where the content dictates that A+B=C. In [Black Girls United] students got to explore how they *feel* about that equation!" (Tanya, Interview #2, December 22, 2012)

When I interviewed Ashanti, she agreed with Tanya's assertion that most high school classes did not offer students opportunities to reflect deeply on their feelings about the curriculum. My English classes were an exception to the rule; I frequently requested that learners share their personal opinions and sentiments in their analyses of the mandated readings. Despite my efforts, Ashanti, a former BGU member, and one of my Honors English students, was hesitant to develop an emotional connection to the majority of the literature in my Honors English class. Yet, Ashanti passionately engaged with the curriculum in Black Girls United. In the following quote, she offers an explanation:

> As far as in class you'd be like, "Should I raise my hand? Naw, I don't really care about what's going on anyway with this subject or with this

book." When I was reading a boring book in English class I was just like "I really don't care. What time is the bell going to ring?" And I wasn't bored *all the time* in yo' class, you know. Some of them readings was cool. But in [BGU] I was *always* into it. It got way deep. Fast. Cuz of the subjects we was talkin' about. It got, it got gritty. And students *wanted* to get emotional in [BGU] cuz [emotion] really was like the base of everything, *like the core of it*. You didn't have to hold back. (Ashanti, Interview #2, December 1, 2012)

It was not uncommon to find literature that was either (a) relevant, (b) current, or (c) emotionally stimulating in a typical class at King High School. However, it was the sophisticated interplay of *all three* characteristics in the literary texts in BGU that incited many highly charged, intellectually charged lunch conversations. In addition to introducing participants to *critical feminist literature, positioning students as change agents* was another structural feature of Black Girls United that ran counter to the norm.

Positioning Students as Change Agents

In Black Girls United, one of my chief objectives was for students to take ideological control over their budding race and gender identities, to access the "elusive sphere of freedom" that womanist philosophers have coined "self-definition" (Collins, 2000, p. 112). Chapter Four revealed how a variety of outside forces triggered profound feelings of powerlessness and vulnerability within BGU participants (e.g., unequal access to social and economic resources, as well as ubiquitous messages of African American girls and women's inferiority). In response to the subjugation that young Black women at King High were experiencing, I aspired to create an empowering *safe space* for these youth. I was prudent in my efforts to construct a liberatory learning environment, and I aimed at utilizing my classroom as a vehicle through which individuals could showcase their leadership capabilities, intellectual aptitude, and resourcefulness. I gauged the overall success of the program through my assessment of the learners' engagement during each meeting and casual conversations with several of the participants.

One example of *positioning students as change agents* was the vital role that the members of BGU played in the development, organization, and direction of the program. In my interview with Nia, she illuminated the importance of "providing students with *both* structure and autonomy" (Nia, Interview #2, December 8, 2012). As discussed in the previous section, there was a set structure in place in Black Girls United, which I clearly articulated in the informational handout that I distributed to potential members. Students were expected to complete the readings for each class, attend our weekly meetings, and actively work towards Black women's social and academic advancement. Likewise, Black Girls United learners were the face of the program and at the center of its operations. I consulted students regarding the curriculum (i.e., themes for discussion and corresponding literature), they held office (i.e., President, Vice President, Secretary), and the participants of BGU facilitated each meeting. Situating students as leaders had a positive influence on their overall self-concept. In my second interview with Tanya, she reflected on the structure of the program:

> I used to hate when clubs had teachers doing everything. They made all the decisions and it was like, man, who is this for, *me or you*? But [BGU] was about the students, and we did everything by ourselves. You were more so like a *helper*. And that is how it should be. It was *our* program. And takin' over as leaders gave us the power. It made us feel powerful. (Tanya, Interview #2, December 22, 2012)

In addition to developing the structure of Black Girls United *alongside* students, my efforts to position members as change agents were revealed in the makeup of our weekly convening's. In BGU, we dialogued about myriad issues that students—and Black women and girls in general—were experiencing in their personal lives as social and political beings. The purpose of our discourse was for the participants to move beyond simple explorations of these issues; it was equally critical for BGU members to formulate practical solutions to the topics that we examined collectively. As such, I assisted the facilitators in designing lessons that would satisfy both ambitions (analyzing the problem and locating resolutions).

It is necessary to note that during these conversations, I rarely offered my personal opinions. When I did verbally participate, moreover, I generally followed the Socratic Seminar method of asking questions that I felt would push students to think about the subject in new ways. Hence, BGU learners developed critical interpretations of their socio-cultural experiences without an adult coercing them to think, feel, and behave in a particular manner. The following vignette demonstrates how my Black feminist pedagogical framework positioned members as change agents. Students were (a) empowered as leaders as they governed the direction of our class discussion, and (b) they challenged each other to move through and beyond their subordination as African American women, to locate opportunities for self and community transformation.

"I Want a Girl with Extensions in Her Hair"

It was the twenty-second week of Black Girls United and the typical lunchtime routine ensued. Students assembled into my classroom alone, or in pairs, anxiously awaiting the discussion of the week. At the last meeting, everyone was instructed to read two texts: "The Black Beauty Myth" by Sirena J. Riley, which appears in the anthology *Colonize This!* and the lyrics of LL Cool J's classic rap song, "Around the Way Girl" (1990). My goal was for students to contrast Riley's examination of the impact of Eurocentric standards of beauty on the body image ideologies of African American women, with LL Cool J's love poem, expressing his intense affection for Black girls from the hood. By this time, we were several weeks into the second semester of BGU and students were familiar with the Socratic Seminar method that guided our conversations. Each week a new facilitator challenged peers to think critically by engaging them in a series of open-ended questions in order to encourage exploration and divergent thinking over simply locating the "right" answer.

As students settled in, I took my usual seat in the director's chair. The thunderous base of LL Cool J's "Around the Way Girl" blared in the background alongside a sea of melanin-rich bodies in red shirts swaying in unison to the melodic tune. Over the course of a 20-minute lunch period, students in BGU began to unearth the discursive production of Black girls and women's inferiority in popular media, specifically relating to traditional notions of beauty. Class commenced as the facilitator, Andrea, addressed the room with a quote from the text:

Andrea (facilitator):	So the quote says, "White women give themselves too much credit when they assume that Black women still want to look like them." So the author … um, Riley … is arguing that Black women … *nowadays* … aren't … *necessarily* following White beauty standards. So, she says that we have our own, separate standards that we are tryin' to meet. What do ya'll think about that?
Loreal:	[Her left hand darts in the air] Nope. I think that's a *lie*!
Andrea (facilitator):	It's a lie? Ok, why?
Loreal:	I actually read that part, and no, I don't agree because … well, I don't know what city *she* lives in, but all these Black girls at [King] are walkin' around with pressed hair and weaves, tryna look like White girls! [Side chatter ensues, and some students respond with "yep"]
Chloe:	[Standing] Yes, and check me out. My weave is new. And I'm cute! But I ain't hardly trying to look like no *White* girl! [Class laughter]
Loreal:	Well *who* you trying to look like? Who has straight hair? And your weave is blonde too! [Class laughs]
Chloe:	I'm trying to look like myself! What's wrong with adding a little extra hair? Ya'll do it too!
Diane:	Cuz you addin' that *good hair*! Why don't you add some nappy hair? [Laughing] I'd pay money to see [Chloe] with some nappy hair in her head! [Class erupts in laughter and side chatter]
Loreal:	*Oh no she didn't say good hair*! I *hate* that term! Hair is hair! Just cuz somebody's hair is straighter than others' don't mean they have good hair! *God* didn't say straight hair is good! He just gave you a certain type. And that don't mean yours is better than mine!
Andrea (facilitator):	Well, *somebody* said straight hair is better than nappy hair! So … if *God* didn't say it, then let me ask ya'll … *who* said it then? Where did the whole, good hair vs. nappy hair come from?

| Kennisha: | From the beginning of time. Slavery. The mixed Blacks, the Blacks who looked more White ... um, they stayed in the house, while *my* ancestors was in the fields pickin' cotton! If you look more White, you—like, you get treated better in this world. Even today, all these um advertisements, and all these commercials with Black actresses and singers and stuff, they *all* look White! Wearing weaves, perming they hair, and getting nose jobs just to be on TV! [Several students applaud and snap their fingers in agreement] |
| Chloe: | Yo, she right tho'. [Rises to her feet] Cuz when I wear my weave [Swinging her hair from right to left], I get love from *all* these dudes up here! So I blame it on society! They *brainwashed* me! And they brainwashed these little boys! [Class laughs] |

In the conversation above, several students disagreed with Riley's assertion that Eurocentric notions of beauty no longer heavily influence the body image philosophies of contemporary African American women. Andrea first referenced the "good hair versus nappy hair" construct to highlight self-hate within the Black community, and then she questioned the cause of its pervasiveness. In response, Kennisha cited the U.S. system of slavery as the foundation for ideologies that privilege *Whiteness* and subordinate women of African origin. Although several of these students recognized and critiqued interlocking forms of oppression inherent within American social and political structures, early in the conversation many failed to recognize their individual agency within these systems. This is apparent in Chloe's comment in which she contended that she is rewarded with positive male attention when she wears blonde hair weaves; she defended her behavior by attributing her decision to straighten her hair on brainwashing by society and young men who spark her interest. Ten minutes of discussion ensued wherein various students cited multiple, legitimate examples of ways they were affected by Eurocentric media images—focusing heavily on their perceived victimization. The following conversation resumed during the point at which our facilitator Andrea became annoyed, interjecting with a comment that challenged her peers to reflect on *their* accountability in perpetuating ideological and behavioral norms.

Andrea (facilitator): Ok, but let's look at the LL song, for example. Ya'll say that Blacks have been brainwashed, but this *brutha* ... LL *Cooool J* ... is feelin' chicks from the hood. With braids, and like cornrows and everything. So, I highlighted this line on the first page: "I want a girl with extensions in her hair—Bamboo earrings, at least two pair." So when he talks about extensions, he's talking about —

Diane and Tina: [Interrupting, in unison] Braids!

Andrea (facilitator): Right, braids, cornrows ... you know, *Black* hairstyles. And he says he wants a girl with bamboo earrings. So, like, he is representin' for girls in the hood. Like *us!* Like—

Kennisha: [Interjecting] And that's nice and all, but he's just *one* man. *One* rapper, who actually appreciates us ... our beauty! Black ways of dress, and nappy hair or whatever. What about the rest of the Black dudes out here? And the rest of the *world?*

Andrea (facilitator): So, are we supposed to hide our natural hair, and natural beauty just cuz the rest of the world doesn't appreciate it? So, then, are there Black women ... like, entertainers, who are weave free, with their *own* noses, [Laughter from the class] who aren't blonde—

Diane: [Yelling from the back of the room] Yeah! My girl Lauryn [Hill]! Oh, and Erykah Badu ... and Jill Scott.

Andrea (facilitator): Ok, she just came up with *three examples* in less than a minute! [Class laughs] And I'm sure there are many more. So, if ... if all these Black women, you know, if they can do it, what's *our* excuse? And like, to keep it real, I'm gonna call myself out here too. Cuz I perm and weave my hair—

Chloe: [Interrupting] But they not *cute* tho! [Several students boo in disagreement]

Diane: What?! They pockets are *fatter than yours*, so they must be doin' something right! That African, *Afrocentric* look is a part of they image and it's making them a *whole* lot of money! I think they are ... just ... *bold!* And we ain't! They makin' that choice even though they working in a industry run by White people! *Controlled* by Whites! So ... we have the choice—just like they do—to wear our

hair natural ... or nappy or whatever you want to call it.
We just livin' in *fear*!

Andrea (facilitator):   Fear of what?

Diane: Fear of *rejection*!

Because one key element of my Black feminist pedagogical framework was to *position students as change agents*, facilitators were instructed to move their peers beyond simply critiquing oppressive social conditions and push them to develop (individual and collective) transformative ideologies and behaviors. In light of this objective, Andrea challenges the group to think of successful Black women in the media who wear their hair in its textured, coily state. Diane immediately recalled several examples and came to the conclusion that women such as Lauryn Hill and Jill Scott have made the conscious, valiant choice to reject Eurocentric standards of beauty in an industry historically controlled by White individuals and White theoretical and social conventions. These women's willingness to embrace a more Africentric[3] image in an appearance-driven industry led Diane to believe that many Black girls are *fearful* of taking the same risk in their everyday lives.

As class concluded, two students experienced self-critical revelations that empowered them to begin resisting popular commercial influences.

Ms. Lane: I think you raise a good point, [Diane]. This idea that our fear takes away our agency. Our *choice*. Because I'm not sure that every Black woman with straight hair is trying to look White, or *be* White. Women, we love versatility. So many of us, you know? [Many students nod in agreement] But when we're walkin' around *fearful* of showing our true colors ... runnin' away from our natural beauty ... our *gifts*—then that's a problem! Living in that kind of fear is a *problem*. And I agree that it is certainly a sign of brainwashing.

Andrea   You better *preach* Ms. Lane! [The class laughs] Ok then ya'll. Ok
(facilitator): so we gotta hurry. Ok let's hurry up cuz the bell about to ring. What I want to know is what are we going to *do* about it? I'm not trying to live in fear forever! [Joking] But forreal, why should I believe that my—my natural hair is *a bad thing*. Like, my natural *texture*. You know, it is brainwashin'. Like [Diane] was sayin', it's fear, you know. If *my girl* Lauryn Hill can rock dreads, then I can! Well, hold up ... . [Class laughs] I'm not taking it *that far*! But ...

	forreal … the next time I get my hair done I'm going to get some of those kinky twists. With highlights. Cute! I'mma spice em' up!
Lynnette:	[Standing from across the room] Oooh, I like those! [Andrea] I should try them with you … yeah, I'll try it out too [Andrea]! [The bell rings, indicating that lunch has come to an end]
Andrea (facilitator):	Ms. Lane, I think we need another week. I have more quotes. I only, I think I only got through, like, half my questions. I have, like, four more questions. It wasn't enough time. We barely got to get into what [Riley] was really tryin' to say. I don't think everybody understood her … um, where she was comin' from. Her point of view.
Chastity:	[Standing up and packing her bags] Yeah, I didn't get to finish reading it, I wanna see where she was going with some of those arguments! [Several students nod in agreement]

After Diane's revelation that numerous African American women are living in fear of rejection, I intervened to ensure that we were not labeling *all* Black women with straightened hair as fearful or as victims of societal brainwashing; rather, I sought for students to look deep within *themselves* to try and determine the roots and influences of their personal body image concepts and behaviors. This led to a particularly noteworthy occurrence that transpired at the end of our discussion: Andrea recognized that she had been socially conditioned to regard her natural hair texture as innately inferior and made a choice to move towards a self-defined concept of beauty. Her decision to take a break from straightening her hair inspired Lynnette, who similarly resolved to experiment with a new, African inspired hairstyle—kinky twists.

After 20 minutes of discussion, the bell rang for the members to conclude their lunchtime activities and head to the next class. By that time, individuals in Black Girls United had clearly articulated a complex understanding and critique of African American women's station within the White American system of beauty; moreover, two individuals were empowered to reject the dominant rhetoric and instead engage in oppositional behaviors and attitudes. As individuals were preparing to leave, Andrea—with backing from several other students—asked for my permission to extend our discussion into the following week. Students' collective, expressed interest in engaging with the text more thoroughly exemplifies high levels of academic engagement as well as a genuine desire for intellectual rigor.

In sum, *positioning students as change agents* involved offering BGU participants ample opportunities to rally in favor of their self-interests, as experts of their socio-political location. Further, learners were tasked to "dream their way into individual and collective freedom" by locating and implementing behaviors that were subversive to their perceived oppression (Sears, 2011, p. 145). In this way, BGU functioned as an alternative and unorthodox space in which students could explore the dialectic of African American women's oppression *and* their activism (Collins, 2000). As the vignette demonstrated, a process of *rearticulation* ensued, wherein the participants' experiences took on new meanings, and some individuals developed an alternative view of themselves and the world (Collins, 2000). Working strategically to *position students as change agents* was due, in most part, to the politicized ethic of care that I engendered as a Black feminist educator, and by proxy, the intense affection that I held for my students and their communities.

A Politicized Ethic of Care

"Fo-Real" Love

> I knew you cared about us. Like really cared because you were always there to help us. We didn't even have to ask a lot of the time cuz, you'd be like, "You look tired [Tanya]. You hungry? You want some carrots?" And then you'd go to the fridge lookin' for some food. Or just, like, you'd see somebody just wasn't their usual self and you would step away from everybody and talk to that person separately. You know? You went out of your way. Or if somebody was havin' family drama you would ask about how they were doin'. Or even being nosey and asking about people's grades all time. Just checkin' in with people all the damn time. It was about showin' concern. Like, you were uncomfortable when we were unhappy. It made you uncomfortable. Or, like, even if we came to you about a problem and you didn't have the answer we knew we could come to you anyway cuz you always connected us with whoever had the answer. (Tanya, Interview #2, December 22, 2012)

Through an analysis of Black feminist curricula, in-class video footage, student artifacts, and interviews with former participants, the students in Black Girls United exposed the ways in which educators at King High School regularly displayed inauthentic forms of caring. From the students' perspectives, many of their teachers were emotionally disconnected, and they did not regard urban youth of color as a valuable investment of their time or worthy of sincere affection. Consequently, the behaviors of these alleged uncaring faculty contributed to the overwhelming sense of invisibility that the members of Black Girls United commonly experienced at school.

Contrastingly, my teaching practice in Black Girls United was anchored by an authentic love and concern for the social and educational well-being of every student. In my second individual interview with a former member named Tanya, she described my disposition towards students in Black Girls United as an "actual and *fo'real* love." When I asked Tanya to elaborate, she responded with the opening excerpt. From her standpoint, my efforts to provide individuals with the necessary supports to thrive in both their personal and academic lives (e.g., academic and emotional support, rides to school, home visits, feeding students, and frequent check-ins), was evidence that I truly cared for the BGU members.

Similar to other Black feminist educators, I exhibited care through the custom of othermothering (Collins, 2000). That is, sharing mothering responsibilities and exhibiting authentic concern for students' holistic development beyond the bounds of the classroom. In my conversations with the participants of BGU, numerous individuals attributed their improved schooling behaviors, at least in part, to the *affective* pedagogical traits that I engendered. In the following transcript, Ashanti recalled how my efforts to provide a wake-up call each morning improved her school attendance. She noted:

> I remember it was on a Friday 'cause I was like this lady ain't gon' call and wake me up, she gon' forget. And I remember that Monday morning you called at like 5 o'clock in the morning. I was pissed when my phone was going, I'm like what?! I'm like she really called my phone, like she really called my phone and woke me up! And it was like after that, every day you called and woke me up and I was on time. Every single day after that I was on time ... Sometimes I just wanted to cut my phone off, but I'd be like I gotta go to school, I gotta go to school ... . You took the time out of your busy mornin'

to call me. Like, it kind of made me open my eyes a little more or kind of push me. Made me want to do better. (Ashanti, Interview #2, December 1, 2012)

Calling Ashanti each morning provided the push that she needed to attend her classes regularly and on time. As her teacher, I was not surprised by the shift in Ashanti's behavior considering the persistent, disempowering schooling conditions that Black girls regularly confronted at King High School. The motherly love and daily wake up calls that originated in my English class continued throughout Ashanti's two-year tenure in Black Girls United—which resulted in a lasting closeness between us.

As a Black feminist educator, I also inherited the convention of shared responsibility, which was glaringly apparent in my critique of BGU participants' physical health and eating patterns. Similar to most teenagers, many of the young women in BGU battled fatigue and low levels of energy. I often informed students that they could attribute their recurrent lethargy to inadequate sleep and terrible food choices. On any given day, I would encounter BGU participants (and other students at King High, in general) devouring Hot Cheetos, Top Ramen Noodles with Tobasco Sauce, and excessive amounts of refined sugar. I often harassed students: "You can't be any good to anybody else, if you can't be good to yourself" (BGU class, Week 49). I was concerned that these young women would fall short of meeting their prestigious career goals, providing for their families, and engaging in meaningful community work if they consumed food that limited their brain function—or if they developed a serious illness (e.g., type 2 diabetes).

After months of pestering students, one member of BGU decided that altering her eating habits was extreme; however, she offered to accompany me on my after-school jogs. I routinely ran on a treadmill at home, but because students were volunteering to join me, we decided to jog around the local neighborhood. Tanya described this tradition during her second interview:

We were in our second year of [BGU] and you were *still* bothering us about the Hot Cheetos. So finally I was like listen, I can't give up my good food, but I'll come run with you. And then, we told some other people and they joined in! And we was committed to it too! Like, you don't see high school students doing that. Like, "Uh, its afterschool, and I'm ready to go home!" But, like we were willing to be together after school to do this together and laugh about it. Joke about it, you know. And that hill was hard! And on the way back we'd be lazy and we'd be walking back. But you made us finish! (Tanya, Interview #2, December 22, 2012)

The testimonies offered by the young women in Black Girls United provide insight into the kinds of caring dispositions and behaviors that young African American women respect and value among educators in urban schools—which, in turn, lead to more positive educational outcomes and attitudes. In addition to caring about students holistically, high levels of student and teacher accountability were integral to my *politicized ethic of care*.

Love Ain't Always Warm & Fuzzy: Reflections on Student Accountability

Chrisette: You *love* us, huh Ms. Lane?

Ms. Lane: [Looking down at papers on the desk] Yes ma'am.

Chrisette: Mmmhmm. *I know. Why* you love us? [Joking] You know we *crazy*, right?!

Ms. Lane: [Looking away, shuffling papers on the desk] You're funny, [Chrisette]. I love you because it comes with the territory.

Chrisette: [Laughing] What territory? Teachin'?

Ms. Lane: Mmmhmm. [Smiling and looking up at Chrisette] It is *literally* my job to love you. [Pointing to the door] Now get to class punkin'.

The above conversation took place after a Black Girls United meeting that was held a few weeks into the second year of the program (BGU meeting, Week 45). One of the benefits of video recording our sessions is that I was able to capture conversations between BGU members and myself that happened just before and immediately following our gatherings. This particular discussion occurred at the close of our lunchtime gathering, as the young women were departing to the next period. When Chrisette walked over, I was sorting through a stack of papers that I had prepared for the students in my next class. However, when she asked me if I loved her BGU peers, I responded instinctually. I answered "yep" without missing a beat and affectionately directed her to get to class.

Numerous scholarship have exhibited how Black women educators embody a complex working of politicized caring, which foregrounds bringing the same standards of care and accountability to one's students as she would to her own children (Beauboeuf-Lafontant, 2002, p. 73). Accordingly, African American women teachers often engender an overt, tough love—fully recognizing that it may pose a threat to their popularity. My exchange with Chrisette provides the perfect introduction into an examination of Black women teachers' high levels of commitment to and expectations for the students they serve. Although I openly communicated my love for Chrisette and her peers, I straightforwardly ushered her to go to class, invoking the "familiar and familial mother-child relationship" that Black women often exercise in their interactions with students (Beauboeuf-Lafontant, 2002, p. 74).

In my individual interviews with a sub-sample of seven Black Girls United members, the participants described past experiences with other effective African American women teachers, and reported that these women also performed caring in ways that were strict, yet heartfelt. For instance, Black women practitioners characteristically went above and beyond the call of duty (i.e., providing rides to school, making home visits, and feeding students), and were often labeled as pushy and loving. A BGU member named Tanisha asserted that African American women educators stayed "on yo' head." These teachers frequently questioned students' whereabouts, monitored individuals' academic progress, and confronted youth who engaged in harmful social behaviors—thereby embodying a "no nonsense" motherly affection. In my practice, I regularly jeopardized my "cool points" with BGU members, opting to engage the young women in difficult conversations that I hoped would evolve the limits of their abilities. As Duncan-Andrade (2009) acknowledges, educators who prioritize being liked often avoid unpleasant encounters with young people, and ultimately jeopardize the social and intellectual potential of students.

An encounter that I had with Ashanti during the second year of the program best exemplifies Duncan-Andrade's sentiment. It was not atypical for students to gather in my room during lunch on days that BGU did not meet. I traditionally played music, graded papers, and conversed with individuals during the half hour break. When Ashanti walked into my classroom she looked at me coldly and sat down in a seat directly in front of my desk. In place of her usual greeting, Ashanti stared directly at me and demonstrated an uncharacteristically uptight disposition. When I probed about the cause of her behavior, Ashanti insisted that nothing was wrong, quietly ate her food, and grimaced in my direction for the remainder of the break.

At the end of the lunch period, I pulled Ashanti aside and encouraged her to speak with me straightforwardly. I told her that if she had a problem with me that she needed to be mature and discuss it like a young adult. She immediately defended her actions by insisting that she did not have an attitude, and managed to mumble an obligatory "I'm sorry." Instead of accepting Ashanti's apology, I communicated that her actions were unacceptable and disappointing. I insisted that she pull herself together and provide a real apology when she was ready to acknowledge her rude behavior. The following day, Ashanti walked into my room at lunch and placed a handwritten card on my desk. She had folded a piece of white printer paper in half and wrote "I Love You" in bold, colorful lettering on the front. On the inside, she taped a recent picture of herself. Opposite the image was a note that read:

Dear Ms. Lane,

I would like 2 apologize for what I did the other day. I never meant to make you feel that what I did was a "punk ass move." And I understand that. So, I'm giving you what you asked for, a "REAL" apology and I hope you will accept it. So for the last time, I'M SORRY MS. LANE!!!

P.S. I also want to thank you for everything you've done for me. You have done more for me then some of my family members and I've been around them my whole life. You've taught me things that I never known and you help me make better choices in life. Ms. Lane, you treat me as if I'm more than just a student 2 u and anything I ever asked you 2 do you did and I really appreciate that. So I don't NEVER want you 2 feel that I don't appreciate what you've done for me because I do.

Love always,
[Ashanti]

The movement in Ashanti's consciousness from denial to self-reflection was emblematic of the reciprocal nature of our relationship. As evidenced by her touching letter, Ashanti recognized that my high expectations for her were also tied to sacrifice and support on my part. In Rochelle Brock's *Sista Talk*, the author endeavored to interpret the central factors in good teaching of Black women to Black women. Her analysis emphasized the importance of "accountability within an ethic of caring," revealing that both are "qualities of effective/affective teaching" (Brock, 2010, p. 108). Through my relentless nurturing and demands for excellence, Ashanti and I had developed a closeness with mutual respect and personal responsibility at the core.

It is critical to note that Black women educators' *politicized ethic of care* does not necessarily result in immediate successes. My experience with Ashanti demonstrates how liberatory teacher pedagogies are subject to student acknowledgement that is congratulatory, although fleeting. As Beauboeuf-Lafontant (2002) warns, "the struggle is long and social in nature ... one cannot egocentrically base one's commitment on seeing instantaneous change" (p. 84). Hence, African American women teachers who embody a *politicized ethic of care* are anchored to the profession by their faith in the power and potential of an enduring social justice praxis. These exemplars lead with a fiery embrace of the maternal, an obligation to transgress social injustice, and an eagerness to assist in the social and intellectual development of their students along the way.

In sum, Black women teachers who espouse a *politicized ethic of care* have the qualities to draw from students' cultural frameworks, lived experiences, socio-emotional needs, and diverse learning styles. This framework is inherently *political* because these educators aim to transform power hierarchies in the interests of a democracy that includes all segments of society. Additionally, Black women's political lucidity is tied to their *emotional* investment in the students they serve. This emotional investment is demonstrated through an authentic form of caring, that includes a love for self and community, othermothering, and teaching the whole child. The *politicized ethic of care* that I exhibited gave rise to the collective participation that was at the core of student relations in Black Girls United.

Collectivity

A Community of Queens

Nia (facilitator):	I mean, I wonder what you guys think about this. I notice that in most videos the so-called "pretty" girl is a light skinned chick who is treated respectfully, and she gets to walk around with the guy. And the other girl, the dark girl, she's not so pretty, but she's *shakin it*. And the next scene is, the guy has sex with the dark skinned girl, *leaves her*, and goes home to wifey … *the light chick*! Is it just me, or have you guys noticed that too? Cuz when you watch videos it's like watching a movie, and when we watch movies we think that's real life. We accept it, like "well, this is real life," sooo … the more we accept it the more it actually *does* take place in real life. And when we see these guys using the dark girls for sex only, but valuing the light girls to where those are the ones worth marrying. Then what—well, *how* does that make us think about ourselves as dark girls? Or, as light-skinned girls?
Ashanti:	[Nodding head] That's true.
Karrine:	Preach! [Raising her arms in the air and snapping her fingers]
Ashanti:	Yep! Preach [Nia]! [Snapping her fingers]
Nia:	[Bell rings] I'm not *tryna* preach, I was *tryna* ask a question! [Laughter from class]
Ashanti:	Well, look, we'll answer yo' question *next time* girl! Let us give you yo props! You did a good job! Everybody, show yo' love for [Nia]! [Ashanti stands and begins clapping. The entire class claps for Nia, while four students and Ms. Lane give a standing ovation along with Ashanti]
Nia (facilitator):	[Shaking her head from left to right and looking around the class] Ya'll are *so* dramatic. [Smiling] Stop clapping *right now*! [Laughing] *For real*!

When students joined Black Girls United, they were implicitly supporting the objective to acquire a sense of sisterhood, cultural appreciation, critical consciousness, and transformative agency. The student information sheet, which I distributed to individuals on the day of the orientation, plainly communicated these ambitions. Truthfully, at the start of BGU most participants did not have a complete understanding of the terms "critical consciousness" and "transformative agency," although they were briefly defined in the handout. In my interviews with seven former members, moreover, numerous individuals admitted that they were initially unclear about how we'd engage in cultural appreciation. To my surprise, the single objective that was unambiguous to students was the sisterhood that we hoped to achieve. Aside from the informational handout, I never explicitly clarified how we would nurture this sisterhood. However, from the very first meeting of Black Girls United, the young women assembled in the spirit of love, encouragement, and uplift.

Through my analysis of data, I determined that there were a few specific reasons why the spirit of collectivity emerged so seamlessly in Black Girls United. First, students were working towards the common goals of self-definition and community empowerment. Secondly, although there were leadership positions within BGU, the members did not identify hierarchies within the program (i.e., a chain of command among students). Lastly, several additional features of BGU were embedded into the structure and set-up of the program—and inspired a sense of solidarity.

In the opening transcript, the participants of Black Girls United exhibited tremendous gratitude after Nia (the facilitator) shared a particularly insightful comment. Although Nia did not anticipate such positive feedback—she became quite embarrassed—her peers insisted on showering her with praise by applauding and shouting "preach" (BGU Class, Week 24). During my interview with Kenya, I asked her why she thought her classmates were so much more supportive of each other in BGU than in traditional classes at King High. In response, she maintained that in Black Girls United, the students had a "purpose that was bigger than themselves":

> There was a kind of *togetherness* in [BGU]. It wasn't like other classes where you think, "I'm doing my thing and she's over there doing her thing." You know? In [BGU], it was like … it was more like, we're doing the same thing, *together*. You know? We all had something in common. We all wanted to do better as Black young women *and* for ourselves, and that was clear. That was the *point* of the program. So there was no real reason to be mean to the next person. We were *all* in it … *together*. (Kenya, Interview #2, January 12, 2013)

As Kenya asserted, Black Girls United members frequently displayed empathy and care towards their peers, which contributed to the atmosphere of "togetherness." Assertions obtained from my individual interviews with Nia and Erykah corroborated Kenya's experiences. Nia recalled how the BGU learners shared an inherent responsibility to "uplift" each other, despite their varied "income levels" and "walks of life" (Nia, Interview #2, December 8, 2012). Moreover, Erykah was particularly appreciative of the high levels of empathy and thoughtfulness expressed by her peers during our weekly meetings. She explained:

> I feel like we lifted each other up when needed. Like, we were all so different and so alike at the same time. But when someone had a personal experience and they were sharing it and they would get emotional, we would all just have that moment of silence and just hug and comfort one another—which I felt was really good. And we just would learn from the different experiences people had. Everybody was welcomed to share. Nobody was thought of as weird or an outcast or nothin'. In my other classes if a student was emotional people would just stare at you like "Okay, why is she crying?" But in [BGU] it was just an aura of sisterhood and support. Everyone knew that's what it's about. We're all *one*, so why put down one another when we could lift each other up?

As Erykah affirmed, the participants welcomed each other with open arms in Black Girls United. As such, young women who were shunned in spaces outside of our program felt "socially accepted" in BGU (Kenya, Interview #2, January 12, 2013). In my conversations with previous members of the organization, the participants agreed that the absence of social hierarchies in BGU also contributed to the development of sisterhood and deep personal attachments among the members. She noted:

> You know what? We didn't really have power hierarchies. There was no competition. Like, *for what*?! Because we was about a sisterhood. Any student could lead, you know? It was whoever volunteered, or whoever was volunteered by somebody else. And if you felt you needed support you could lean on the president or vice president for support. And anybody was able to give ideas about what we *could* be doin' or *should* be doin in the program. It always seemed like everybody was all together. It was a even playing field. You just had to be Black and female, basically. (Tanya, Interview #2, January 22, 2012)

Valuing *collectivity* over competition was a key component of my Black feminist pedagogical framework because it prevented students from mirroring the social hierarchies they experienced outside of the program. In Black Girls United, African American young women were not stratified based on appearance, popularity, grades, or alleged misbehavior. On the contrary, there was a true "sense of oneness" among the students (Tanya, Interview #2, December 22, 2012).

Although Black Girls United was a student organization, it played a vital role in the BGU sisterhood. The members affectionately nicknamed me "mama Lane," "mom," and "Auntie Mo," despite their acknowledgment of my positionality as "the adult in charge" (Ashanti, Interview #1, October 10, 2012). Because the BGU participants facilitated the weekly conversations—and we *co-constructed* the curriculum—I practically felt like an equal participant. Moreover, as revealed in previous sections of this chapter, I did not speak very often during the Black Girls United meetings. Although, when I contributed, I posed thoughtful questions that encouraged learners to uncover their assumptions and analyze concepts more deeply.

On other occasions, I commiserated with students by sharing examples from my personal or professional life, revealing the ways in which I have grappled with the diverse discussion topics. For instance, when we read *How Sexual Harassment Slaughtered, Then Saved Me* by Kiini Ibura Salaam (2002), I disclosed the trauma and powerlessness that I experienced as a teenager as I watched my mother endure a vicious cycle of domestic abuse (BGU class, Week 36). As Jeff Duncan-Andrade (2009) declared, to be a true critical educator means that one "painfully examines their own lives and actions within an unjust society and [share] the sensibility that pain may pave the path to justice" (p. 7). I believed that exposing my humility and humanity would stimulate BGU members' processes of ideological transformation. Therefore, I was open, honest, and vulnerable alongside the participants. As a result, our conversations often felt like "girl talk, only deeper" (Ashanti, Interview #2, December 1, 2012).

There were additional features of Black Girls United that contributed to our sense of *collectivity*. First, I arranged the seats in my classroom in a U shape, or semi-circle, which I believed was integral to engaging in democratic conversations. The facilitator typically chose to lead at the opening of the U (which was the front of the classroom), roughly two feet in front of a large whiteboard. Moreover, to encourage collectivity within the organization—it was a tradition for each member, including myself, to wear our bright red Black Girls United shirts at each meeting. The word "Queen" was written in bold, cursive lettering across the front of our shirts, with our logo on the back in a colorful red, black, and green pattern. Primarily, our BGU shirts functioned as a reminder of our rich ancestry, intellectual talents, and inherent overall greatness. In my interviews with former students, several individuals maintained that our shirts served an extraordinary purpose in the program. My conversation with Lisa confirmed this notion (Interview #2, January 4, 2013):

Ms. Lane:	So how did you feel about the red queen shirts with the black "Queen" written across the top?
Lisa:	It was empowering.
Ms. Lane:	Oh really? Why?
Lisa:	Because of what it represented. Like, you are a *queen*. You are valued, you're respected. Like, you're strong. [Laughing] And it's like solidarity, we're in this together. Like we have our … we're in this together. Like *self-love*, like in that song, what's the song? [Singing] "*Self-love* … "
Ms. Lane:	[Singing] "*Self-preservation*." Yeah, by Jaguar Wright.
Lisa:	Yea, that whole thing.
Ms. Lane:	Did it make you feel differently?
Lisa:	I mean yea it does, it made us, well it made *me* remember that I was royalty. So it's just like, it was a mind thing, like you know how a lot of times the more you see something, it kinda embeds itself. So in your mind having a shirt that said "Queen" with the, the um African stuff on the back, it just reminded me like, "Okay well, you're a queen, so you to behave yourself as such." And then after awhile, it kinda started to really like get to the mind. Like, okay well if you *act* like you're royalty—not like snotty and you know like things like that—but it's just like, if you act like it, sometimes you just gotta fake it 'til you make it. *And eventually it'll become embedded in you.* And you'll realize that you were worth more than how other people may treat you. Or even worth more than you think you are to yourself. So um, yeah, I like the shirts. I think the shirts were tight.

Ms. Lane:	I like that, "fake it 'til you make it." It'll eventually sink in. Ok, so what kind of reactions would you get at school?
Lisa:	Yeah … a lot of questions. Because I mean, you would see one of us, and it was like, "Ok well, she has on her red queen shirt, that's something she went and got made." But as they would see more of us like okay, *"Queen again?!"* Then it's like they'll stop like, "Hey, where did you get that shirt from" or "What does this mean? What's [BGU]?" And then I'd tell them "Oh we talk about women issues and being Black and stuff," then they'd want to know more about what we used to talk about and do in class and stuff. Being nosey [Laughing]. And then it was actually interesting because it not only drew the young ladies' attention but it drew the males' attention as well. So I mean, it gave us some opportunity to talk about the program.
Ms. Lane:	So would you say the overall response from your peers was positive or negative or somewhere in the middle? What would you say?
Lisa:	From the things that I experienced, I thought that it was positive. Now I'm not necessarily sure if it was because we were doing something different, something outside of cheerleading, and sports, or just tryin' to be cute getting bad grades. Or like, a wannabe video chick. I don't know what was in they heads for sure. But for me, I felt like they thought it was something positive. I think people were thinking … it gave people a *different* type of perception of what Black girls stood for. We were outside the box, you know?
Lane:	So it gave people a different image of the Black girl at [King]? And it sounds like some folks were intrigued by it?
Lisa:	*Exactly.*

As Lisa reported, the Queen shirts were a symbol of respect, honor, and strength for the young Black women in BGU. According to my former students, this representation subverted the dominant narrative about African American girl learners as hypersexual and unintelligent. Furthermore, the Queen shirts garnered numerous inquiries from other students on campus and were frequently the cause of the positive attention that the young women received on Thursdays. During my conversations with former members—which took place two-to-four years after their high school graduation—I learned that three of the seven interviewees had held onto their shirt. Surprisingly, Kenya wore her shirt to our interview.

In addition to the Queen shirts, there were several activities outside of school that deepened the bond between the members of Black Girls United. As previously mentioned, we participated in weekly jogs during the second semester of the final year of the program. We also visited a theme park, attended a concert and a community rally, and participated in King High School's homecoming parade. By and large, the general sense of *collectivity* that Black Girls United members encountered had a particularly powerful and lasting impact on several of the learners.

Conclusion: In Love *and* War

Together, the foundational components of *critical feminist literature, positioning students as change agents, a politicized ethic of care,* and *collectivity* gave rise to an alternative safe space for the African American girl learners in Black Girls United. While the previous sections have illuminated specific strategies and approaches to teaching that resulted in an extraordinarily stimulating urban classroom environment, it is imperative to mention that there were also instances of discord among individuals in BGU. Many of the topics covered in our weekly meetings ignited passionate responses from the members. Brittney, a former participant, noted:

> Students had a chance to really listen to one another's stories, and actually learn from each other's experiences. But we didn't think the same, and we didn't always agree. Sometimes it was *super* heated. (Brittney, Interview #1, October 19, 2012).

As Brittney recalled, the young women in BGU had indeed developed a sisterhood; however, they were not a monolithic group, and the learners often disagreed in class. As such, zealousness and conflict were regularly at the heart of our conversations.

I refer to these instances as respectful rifts. Any group working collectively in the spirit of transformational resistance must struggle with *and* against each other, to stimulate a new consciousness and incite oppositional behaviors (Sears, 2011). In the moments where individuals fervently disagreed in Black Girls United, the members of the organization remained courteous. For example, during the second year of the program, the BGU learners engaged in a heated yet civil debate about the inappropriate nature of a trendy rap song (BGU class, Week 36):

Brenda:	Honestly, when I listen to songs, I never feel like they talkin' bout me! [Laughing] I never looked at it like that! I just … be like … the song *tight*! [Laughing] [Several students nod in agreement]
Ashanti:	What about that Too Short song? You know, you don't really think about it, like, damn he talking about females! He's bad mouthing females. And it don't even make sense, really!
Brenda:	*Sadiddy* makes sense. I think—
Ashanti:	[Interrupting, and raising her voice] No it *don't*!
Karrine:	Nuh uh!
Nia:	Hold up, let her talk, [Brenda] how does *Sadiddy* make sense to you? Wait, have you guys all heard that song by Too Short? *Saddidy*? He talks about "You're a saddidy bitch." You went to college but, [Imitating the rapper] "You're actin' all sadiddy *BITCH*!" [Class erupts in laughter]
Ms. Lane:	Oh my, I haven't heard that one. My *goodness*! Let me write this one down! So that's [writing] Too Short, *Saddidy Bitch*. [Class laughs]
Nia:	It's literally just bitches, and bitches, and more bitches.
Brenda:	[Standing] But that's not even his worst! It's actually not that bad, when you think about it.
Nia [Looking at Brenda]:	So *why* do you think *Sadiddy* makes sense?
Brenda:	Cuz you know, people get a education and start to act stuck up and stuff. Why you gotta act like that? You ain't too cute to get slapped! [Laughing]
Ashanti:	Whaaaat?! I can't even listen to this. I gotta admit, I be listening to the song, like, it *do* bang. But how you gon' say it's ok for him to slap a woman across her face cuz' she don't wanna holler at him?
Brenda:	That's one part of the song that I actually like. Out of all the other parts of the song, that one part makes a lotta sense! You ain't *never* too cute to get slapped!
Ashanti:	So, *you* ain't never too cute to get slapped? Yo *mama* ain't too cute to get slapped? [Several students yell "oooh"]
Brenda:	Hold up! [Leaning forward, and frowning] My mama ain't in this. That's *different*.
Nia:	[Raising her voice from across the room] I don't think she's talking about *your* mom, [Brenda]. But if it's not cool to slap

	yo' mama, how's it ok to slap another woman? [Chatter from other members of the class] That could be someone's mama too! That could be *my* mama, or [*Ashanti's*] mama, or—
Ashanti:	[Interrupting] That's all I'm sayin'!
Brenda:	[Taking her seat] Well, I ain't never said it's alright to slap *nobody's* mama. We talkin' about these *bougie* girls, right out of college. But … whatever. I wasn't takin' it like that. I don't think a mother should be slapped. [Laughing] Not even a *baby* mama!
Karrine:	[Interrupting] Look [Speaking to the class], I just think we need to realize how men listen to this and think its ok to copy what he says. And *any* woman could be a victim. Like, what you gon' do if that happens to *you* after you get your degree? Just because you're not down some dude slaps you! *That ain't cool!*
Brenda:	It's like … I mean, I feel you. I just don't think it's right for people to act stuck up. But yeah, I don't want *nobody* touchin' me!

Tensions flared between Brenda and Ashanti when Brenda asserted that no woman is "too cute to get slapped." The debate further escalated when Ashanti mentioned Brenda's mother as an example—to dispute Brenda's claims. As the discussion progressed, students raised their voices, interrupted each other, and grew increasingly uneasy in their seats. Ultimately, the other members of BGU (i.e., Karrine, and Nia) intervened as mediators to keep the conversation focused. Specifically, Karrine and Nia were determined to aid Brenda in pinpointing the connection between the degradation of women in music videos, and real-life romantic partnerships that mirror such behaviors. As Tanya pointed out during our second interview, the BGU learners were negotiating how to "be a Black woman in our society," and "to be successful they had to work together, as siblings" (Tanya, Interview #2, December 22, 2012). Moreover, she asserted, "Siblings bicker, but in the bickering, we made each other better." Hence, conflict and individual and collective accountability were fundamental to an authentic sisterhood.

In sum, my Black feminist pedagogical praxis involved taking on a supportive role and carefully listening to students' narratives—which widened my understanding of African American girl adolescents' multiple and entangled social positionalities. Moreover, through Socratic questioning and a *politicized ethic of care*, I challenged the members of

Black Girls United to puncture feelings of hopelessness and despair; rather, we cultivated a sense of critical optimism about the state of Black femininity and African American girlhood. The dynamic framework and student-centered organizational structure fostered members' intellectual curiosity, agency, and collective empowerment. The next chapter offers a rigorous discussion of how my Black feminist praxis influenced the participants' identity development, in general, and engendered #BlackGirlJoy.

Questions for Deeper Engagement

1. The author maintains that BGU participants' positive responses to the *politicized ethic of care* that she espoused in the organization necessitates African American girl students' increased exposure to these practices. Explore the potential usefulness of an embodied *politicized ethic of care* praxis in conventional K–12 classroom settings.

2. Recent data indicate that Black women educators comprise less than five percent of the nation's public K–12 teachers and White women make up the majority of the teaching force (Feistritzer, 2011). In light of this data, how might White women educators— who do not necessarily have oppressed nationality people to orient themselves to—engage a Black feminist pedagogical framework?

Notes

1 The National Association of Colored Women (NACW) originated in 1896 out of the African American women's club movement. Its founders included Harriet Tubman, Frances E. W. Harper, Ida B. Wells-Barnett, and Mary Church Terrell. The NACW motto, "lifting as we climb" represents the club's aim to empower and uplift all Black women through ambitious and brazen displays of social activism.

2 It is important to note that students were not instructed to complete additional assignments (i.e., homework) apart from the weekly readings. All written work (e.g., free writes, short poems, and handouts) was assigned and fulfilled during our meetings and was utilized strictly for engaging students in discussion. Hence,

I did not grade students' work, or participate in any formal assessment of these assignments. I did, however, retain several exemplars of student work, which I have utilized as potential data sources for this study.

3 *Africentrism* is a worldview relocating values, experiences, and expressions of Black-identified individuals, placing them at the center, rather than at the margins of popular U.S. thought.

References

Bartolomé, L. I. (1994). Beyond the methods fetish: Toward a humanizing pedagogy. *Harvard Educational Review, 64*(2), 173–195.

Beauboeuf-Lafontant, T. (2002). A womanist experience of caring: Understanding the pedagogy of exemplary Black women teachers. *The Urban Review, 34*(1), 71–86.

Brock, R. (2010). *Sista talk: The personal and the pedagogical.* New York, NY: Peter Lang Publishing.

Broussard, C. (1996). *The Black woman's guide to financial independence.* London, UK: Penguin Books.

Collins, P. (2000). *Black feminist thought: knowledge, consciousness, and the politics of empowerment* (2nd ed.). New York, NY: Routledge.

Duncan-Adrade, J. M. R. (2009). Note to educators: Hope required when growing roses in concrete. *Harvard Educational Review, 79*(2), 1–13.

Feistritzer, E. (2011). *Profile of teachers in the U.S. 2011.* Retrieved from http://www.edweek.org/media/pot2011final-blog.pdf

Hansberry, L. (1958). *A raisin in the sun.* New York, NY: Random House.

LL Cool J. (1990). Around the way girl. On *Mama said knock you out* [CD]. New York, NY: Def Jam Recordings.

Luna, S. (2002). HIV and me: The Chicana version. In D. Hernandez & B. Rehman (Eds.), *Colonize this!: Young women of color on today's feminism* (pp. 71–84). Emeryville, CA: Seal Press.

Morgan, J. (1999). *When chickenheads come home to roost: My life as a hip hop feminist.* New York, NY: Simon & Schuster.

Riley, S. J. (2002). The Black beauty myth. In D. Hernandez & B. Rehman (Eds.), *Colonize this!: Young women of color on today's feminism* (pp. 357–369). Emeryville, CA: Seal Press.

Salaam, K. I. (2002). How sexual harassment slaughtered, then saved me. In D. Hernandez & B. Rehman (Eds.), *Colonize this!: Young women of color on today's feminism* (pp. 326–342). Emeryville, CA: Seal Press.

Sears, S. D. (2010). *The negotiation of power and identity within the Girls Empowerment Projects.* Albany: SUNY Press.

Too Short, ft. Lil Jon. (2003). Shake that monkey. On *Married to the game* [CD]. New York, NY: Zomba Recording LLC.

Wilson, A. (1986). *Fences.* New York, NY: Penguin Group.

'One of the things that I love about joy—unlike happiness, which has become a commodity—is that joy can hold misery and pain. Joy can hold the reality of the human experience, while still remaining filled with light.'

~Tracee Ellis Ross

Chapter Six

Engendering #BlackGirlJoy

Reversing the Tide of Young Black Women's Inferiority

real rule makers
true dream chasers
and they can't replace us
but they imitate us
Kim & Kylie wear braids
but they say mine are ghetto
r&b singers call us bitches
in a falsetto
Common says we're queens
kinda hard to believe
cause my teacher laughs
when the whole class clowns my weave
sometimes we insecure
be needin' reminders that we rock

> Black girls anchored to this fight
> and we ain't gon' never stop

Jynné Ross's (2020) poem, "Conflicted," depicts young Black women's struggle to acquire an internally defined outlook of oneself, amidst the disorienting fog of racist and sexist oppression. The poem documents African American girls' intoxicating influence as "real rule makers," and their plight to overcome society's gratuitous objectification. Ross—a poet and entrepreneur—juxtaposes the entitled indifference of those who appropriate Black women's cultural expressions with manifestations of misogynoir (Bailey & Trudy aka @thetrudz, 2018) in contemporary R&B music and within educational institutions. Indeed, the convergence of these violent, joy-eroding forces is the source of intermittent insecurity for Black girl adolescents. Notwithstanding Ross's recognition of African American girls' resilient and active struggle, the author's words also stir a call to conscience about society's determined subjugation of Black women and girls as an entity. Her poetic musings, moreover, illuminate the urgency for U.S. school programming that is restorative and life-affirming.

The purpose of this inquiry was to explore the impact of my Black feminist pedagogical framework on Black Girls United members' race and gender identities. I have discovered that the African American girl-identified students participating in the program underwent a journey comparable to what Ross describes. The BGU learners gathered in fellowship each week, anchored by an unapologetic resolve to deconstruct prevailing notions of Black femininity and celebrate the beauty of African American womanhood. From the students' perspectives, *before* joining Black Girls United, there were few accurate and empowering representations of African American girlhood in their communities and at King High School. Consequently, BGU students' oscillating *invisibility* and *hyper-visibility* resulted in various self-defeating behaviors as a form of resistance (e.g., ditching school).

An analysis of the data has revealed that after two years of participating in Black Girls United, most of the learners agreed with the sentiments expressed by Jynné Ross in the opening poem. That is, the asphyxiating presence of Black women's intertwined race, class, and gender oppression could not be easily unraveled. Fortunately, however, by engaging in a collective process of self-exploration and self-determination, Black Girls United was a vehicle by which students could *begin* to subvert their perceived and experienced oppression.[1] I refer to this undertaking as #BlackGirlJoy, the conscious cultivation of one's identity, purpose, and power. Essentially, the Black feminist pedagogical framework that I employed in BGU invigorated students' imaginations, and they crafted empowered understandings of themselves, which resulted in encouraging social and academic behavioral shifts.

Considering the highly oppressive conditions in which Black Girls United members were socialized and schooled—amidst the maelstrom of adolescence, moreover—learners' movement towards self-discovery is truly worthy of celebration. The following sections reveal three specific areas of growth, which collectively represent BGU students' expression of #BlackGirlJoy: (a) a heightened awareness of African American women's socio-political location, (b) an empowered sense of self that rejected popular, reductive notions of Black femininity, and (c) a more positive orientation towards school. It is important to note that despite the overall success of the program, its impact was limited for one former member. Hence, this chapter concludes with the critical perspective of one participant, whose *joy* was not sustained beyond the bounds of the BGU classroom.

Toward a Consciousness of Connectedness

In the beginning [of Black Girls United] the girls talked about the condition of Black women in general terms. They were aware of racial hierarchies, and classism and sexism—but I believe their perspectives were, for the most part, limited to what they saw happening in their families, with their friends, and in their hoods. I'm not sure that they understood how racism, sexism, classism, and other "isms" unite Black women on a larger scale—in spite of our individual differences and place and space in time. Today, after two years of lovin' on each other, fussin' and cussin', and sharing our stories, I think they finally get it! (Journal 4, Entry 14, p. 61)

Like a monsoon downpour, awe and fulfillment overwhelmed my spirit as I penned the above journal entry. I had recognized—three weeks before the final Black Girls United meeting—that over the two-year span of the program, my students developed a heightened critical awareness of Black women's socio-political location and gratitude for our wide range of diverse experiences. In the early stages of BGU (i.e., Weeks 1–5), the participants shared criticisms of societal threats to African American girls' humanity. The members spoke openly about racial intolerance, economic stratification, and sexism— and how these forms of oppression were hazardous impediments to themselves and their close family and friends. Indeed, an emergent critical consciousness was present for most of the students at the *start* of the organization.

However, what was absent from these early conversations was a clear connection to African American women who lived *outside* of the learners' respective communities and peer groups. Throughout much of the discourse in Black Girls United, students often prefaced their analyses with phrases such as, "When you're a Black girl in South L.A., you get looked at like you're a criminal … " (Andrea, BGU class, Week 2). Or "If you from the eastside, and you a Black female, people treat you like … " (Ashanti, BGU class, Week 4). While students were able to clearly identify African American women's group standpoint early in the program, it wasn't until after *the first semester* of Black Girls United (i.e., after week 15, of a total of 70 weeks) that I began noticing the ways in which the participants' understandings of themselves had expanded to include the experiences of Black women outside of their communities as a criterion of meaning. In my second interview with Erykah, she explained the dramatic shift in her thinking:

Interviewer:	Was there a difference in how you saw yourself as a Black young woman before [BGU] compared to how you felt about yourself at the end of the program?
Erykah:	Yes. Definitely.
Interviewer:	How so? Can you explain? Because you were in … what … the 9th and 10th grade during [BGU], right?
Erykah:	Yep. I was young. [Laughing] In the beginning I really loved being a Black girl and I knew I was special. But, I think … I kind of feel like I didn't really have a good connection to *other* Black women. Not in the beginning. Like, you know, outside of just *my* neighborhood, or my friends. Because, you know,

we kind of lived in a bubble at [King]. And that's all we really knew. And whatever we saw on television, you know. So, I really, honestly believe that those readings helped me to *really* see how crazy racism and sexism are. It's like ... we *knew* it was happening, but ... when you read about other people's lives and they live in other parts of America—because those women were from all over, but they were dealing with problems that I could relate to. It was like ... *it was like looking in a mirror* kind of. And you know, sometimes, new topics were brought up that I hadn't dealt with yet myself, but it increased my knowledge. My knowledge of *Black* women. Because I felt like maybe one day I would come across some of these issues as I get older and really get into the world. So, I learned that being a *Black* woman was more complicated than I thought it was. *We're* complicated. I learned a lot about our lives and how we think about things. I was just a sponge, taking it all in.

Erykah was one of many students whose connection to, and understanding of Black women was significantly broadened by the *critical feminist literature* that they encountered. Through her engagement with the weekly readings, she recognized the variations and commonalities in African American women's life journeys.

Student comparisons of their realities against those of their BGU *peers* was another factor contributing to their expanded perspectives of Black women's collective struggle. As previously mentioned, many of the participants' initial perceptions of African American women were limited to their knowledge of the life experiences of their family members and peers—who often shared similarities in age, social class, sexual orientation, educational histories, religion, and ethnicity. During my analysis of the data, I discovered that in several of the discussions that took place throughout the first and second years of the program, students were surprised to learn of the *diversity* of their lives as urban Black girl adolescents. There were many moments in which individuals' personal truths *contradicted* the experiences of other learners in the organization. It was during these times that students struggled to acknowledge that Black women and girls have "diverse responses to common challenges" (Collins, 2000, p. 25). Students' internal conflict often resulted in heated exchanges, and the participants struggled to re-conceptualize their own beliefs about African American femininity.

These moments of discord between BGU members were critical, as they typically sparked a new, and elevated consciousness.

Omi and Winant (1994) refer to this ideological shift as a process of *rearticulation*. When Black women and girls engage in critical group dialogue, an alternative understanding of themselves and their worlds often emerges. Moreover, altered thinking is accompanied by transformational acts of resistance against oppressive social structures. One powerful example of *rearticulation* in Black Girls United was the evolution of the relationship between two students, Tanisha and Kiera— both of whom were juniors at the start of the program. The root of their friction lied in the young women's perceptions of how race, class, and gender subordination occurred in their individual lives.

Tanisha was a voluble student with a brassy disposition and a deep brown complexion. Her middle-class mother and father raised her in a single-family home, roughly 15 minutes from King High School. Kiera, who was a pecan-colored hue, also lived close by. She and her mother and younger sibling resided in a low-income community of apartment complexes that was deteriorating under the grind of gang violence. Tanisha and Kiera's tumultuous relationship originated in the third week of the program during a heated exchange about the complex and contradictory effects of gentrification. When Ayanna, the facilitator of the discussion, referred to the process of gentrification as "the whitening of yo' neighborhood, like the whitening of yo' teeth" (Ayanna, BGU class, Week 3), Tanisha brazenly asserted that only "darker-skinned Blacks" would be negatively affected by this process, as "light-skinned people" will simply "blend in with the Whites" (Tanisha, BGU class, Week 3). After considering Tanisha's comment, Kiera intervened:

Kiera:	[Looking at Ayanna, the facilitator] Can I say somethin'? Hold on, that's *so* ignorant. That's the most *ignorant* thing I heard all week!
Tanisha:	Ok I'll give an example. Light-skinned girls have it easier cuz people think you less Black, and so you get treated better.
Kiera:	[Tanisha], you're *wrong*! You're not makin' *any* sense right now! You need to get some light-skinned friends cuz' you don't know what you talkin' about.
Tanisha:	I *got* light-bright friends!

Kiera: And all of them are rich? They all live in mansions? They all got
            maids and picket fences, [Tanisha]?
Tanisha: They got more money than *me*!
Kiera: [Interrupting] And *you* got more money than *me*! Explain that!
Tanisha: I don't have money. My parents got money cuz they got jobs.
Keira: Ok but look at where you live tho'. Your parents have more
            money than *my* parents. Are they dark-skinned like you?
Tanisha: Yeah ...
Kiera: [Interrupting] *Exactly*! You're *wrong* [Tanisha].

The discussion between Tanisha and Kiera lasted for 10 minutes. It was the first of many interactions where the young women disagreed about how the forces of racism and social class oppression work in concert with skin-color privilege. Tanisha insisted that Keira's lighter complexion protected her against overt acts of injustice. Because one of the main features of my Black feminist pedagogy was *positioning students as change agents*, I traditionally allowed the young women in BGU to resolve their altercations without broadcasting my personal opinions on the matter. I rarely intervened during quarrels and simply posed questions that required learners to think critically or more carefully. Because Tanisha and Kiera interacted passionately—yet, respectfully— I was not compelled to mediate their quarrel. I was confident in both members' maturity and expected them to reconcile their issues without my assistance.

At long last, during the second semester of the second year of the program, Tanisha had a change of heart. Kiera disclosed a private family matter during one of our weekly meetings: two of her close relatives had endured vicious acts of sexual assault. Kiera's grandmother had been raped by her White employer, and her aunt had been sexually violated by a domestic partner. As a survivor of sexual assault, Tanisha walked away from that meeting with an alternative view of Kiera, and light-skinned Black women in general.

When she returned to my classroom after school, Tanisha explained to me that lighter-skinned Black women's bodies reside on the periphery of discussions about sexual violence, apart from the institutionalized sexual exploitation of African American women during the era of chattel slavery in the United States. She referenced how Black women with lighter complexions were held in high esteem in film and television as well as minority-populated urban communities. Tanisha's limited paradigm had led her to believe that dark and light-skinned women inhabit culturally disparate worlds. Although Tanisha still felt that Kiera was "annoying," she learned from that day's meeting that *all* Black women are vulnerable to acts of racism and sexual malfeasance. I was pleased to hear her admonition, "No matter if you're light skinned or dark skinned, I guess rape don't have a preference" (Journal 3, Entry 4, p. 46). Ultimately, Tanisha recognized that individual variations in how African American women experience sexist exploitation do not overshadow "recurring patterns of differential group treatment" (Collins, p. 26). Several weeks later, I learned that Tanisha volunteered to participate as a guest speaker at a local community forum about the epidemic of sexual violence in the U.S., which disproportionately impacts Black and Latinx women (Journal 3, Entry 11, p. 92). The endeavor was the first of many acts of service and political labor that Kiera would zealously pursue in subsequent years.

In sum, engaging with the *critical feminist literature*—and through the sharing of students' multifaceted personal stories—BGU participants developed a heightened consciousness of African American women's socio-political location as a whole. Because we explored a variety of issues in the program, the members were introduced to topics concerning Black women across the diaspora (e.g., girls and adolescents' genital mutilation in Africa), as well as domestic phenomena that some individuals had not encountered in their own lives (e.g., adoption; child and domestic abuse; extreme poverty and homelessness). As a former student named Tanya asserted during her interview, the young women in Black Girls United "traveled down a path together," eventually concluding that they are "similar *and* different at the same time" (Tanya, Interview #2, December 22, 2012).

Patricia Hill Collins (2000) maintains that one of the many benefits of young Black women gathering in fellowship is that it often leads to novel ideas, which inspires alternate behaviors and ultimately results in new forms of consciousness. Collins writes about the interdependence of action and thought:

> A dialogical relationship characterizes Black women's collective experiences and group knowledge. On both the individual and the group level, a dialogical relationship suggests that changes in thinking may be accompanied by changed actions and that altered experiences may in turn stimulate a changed consciousness. (p. 30)

Essentially, Black Girls United was a lever for inquiry, exploration, and evolution. A collective standpoint emerged as the learners unburied their truths, and shifts in student thought sparked transformative behaviors. One significant outcome of the members' expanded perspectives of Black women was their reimagining of, and ultimate opposition to, reductive notions about African American girls and women's inferiority.

Self-Definition and Coming to Voice

In Chapter 4, I described how the students in Black Girls United were adversely affected by social discourse that malign African American women and girls, including derogatory depictions of themselves in the popular media (e.g., hip-hop music, television, and film). For instance, individuals reported feelings of *hypervisibility,* as a result of their ubiquitous encounters with caricature-like images of Black women as loud, ghetto, hypersexual, and anti-intellectual. In essence, the young women in BGU struggled each day to retain their humanity in the face of these "crooked images" (Harris-Perry, 2011, p. 30). As discussed in the previous section, Black Girls United regularly exposed the participants to counternarratives of African American women that stretched individuals' thoughts about their entangled identities.

In my conversations with former BGU students, they maintained that reading the assigned literature and participating in class discussions sharpened their critical analytical lenses. Nia noted:

> You're looking in between the lines of *everything.* You are not just viewing something on the surface. Everything I started to look at, I was *analyzing.* And questioning. I had to stop myself. Like "Listen Ms. Analyzing, I need you to stop. It is what it is, and you need to let it be. Don't try to find the *bigger picture* and solution to *every single thing*!" But I really couldn't help it. Because you start to analyze magazines, you start to analyze music videos, you start

to analyze music in general, you know. You start to analyze your own sur-roundings. Why are Black women treated like prostitutes in these videos? Why are all the so-called pretty women light? Or the smart women are never Black? Like, you start to analyze things that were happening at school, and *everywhere* really. (Nia, Interview #2, December 8, 2012)

According to the data excerpts, participating in Black Girls United enhanced the learners' critical sensemaking, as they peeled back the layers of the underlying ideologies that shaped their perspectives and social interactions. As Nia pointed out, students began paying closer attention to the over-representation of Black women in discourse and imagery that highlighted cultural pathology. Moreover, the *critical fem-inist literature* and BGU members' storytelling led participants to re-construct Black femininity during their intellectual explorations. For several students, this new angle of vision resulted in their rejection of discursive and symbolic constructions of Black girls as inherently subordinate.

Self-Love and Strident Critiques of Black Girl Adolescent Imagery

Since that meeting about appreciating our natural beauty, [Ayanna] has experimented with so many different hairstyles. I've seen other students compliment her in [BGU]. She has the most gorgeous, thick and kinky hair. She's still quite reserved in 2nd period—sort of sinks into her desk at the back of the class, with her pen and notebook. But I can see a difference in her. There's a light shining from within. Her demeanor has changed. When she comes to [BGU] on Thursdays she walks differently. There's a pep in her step. Shoulders back. Head up. Wearing her afro puff like a crown. "Queen" blasted across her chest. It's beautiful to have participated in her journey. (Journal 3, Entry 4, p. 11)

During the twenty-fourth week of Black Girls United, the members agreed that some African American women sport natural, un-straight-ened hairstyles as a deliberate act of resistance against Eurocentric beauty ideals. Several weeks after that class session, I noticed a signif-icant shift in one student's demeanor. Ayanna, who was both a mem-ber of Black Girls United and one of my ninth-grade English students, was engaging in *self-definition*—an embodied discourse. According to Collins (2000), self-definition occurs when Black women reject external depictions of themselves, and craft identities that foster individual empowerment. Adopting a self-defining stance is often generated by feelings of *self-love*, which involves unconditional care, nurturing, and acceptance of oneself (Sears, 2011). In my interviews with seven former BGU members, I asked each person if they recognized changes in their disposition or outlook, as an outcome of their experience in the program. A stronger sense of self-love and acts of self-definition were common responses amongst the interviewees:

> I was in the high school environment with my peers who didn't like always accept me, so it was hard to love me and be confident. But as far as [BGU] it made me look at myself differently. A little more positively. It gave me a little like, a little spark you know. (Kenya, Interview #2, January 12, 2013)

> I learned that it's ok for others to have an opinion of me, but my own self-concept is what matters most. That it was important for me to love *myself*, no matter what. And that's what matters. (Brittney, Interview #2, December 15, 2012)

> It just was such an empowering thing like this helped me to learn me, to find me, and respect me, *for me*. And accepting myself in the skin that I'm in, and thinking of it like "You are a *beautiful* African American girl," no matter what anybody says. (Tanya, Interview #2, December 22, 2012)

> Yeah, to accept your hair texture mentally and physically. Um, I'll have to say I recognize my self-worth every single day. Like no matter how much someone may disrespect you, just always know your self-worth because it could go a long way. So I think that's the main thing I held on to. Self-love and self-worth. 'Cuz in those videos, Angela Davis, even though she was—you know, going through her spills and people framed her and did everything, she knew her self-worth, and she had self-love. (Erykah, Interview #2, January 19, 2013)

> [BGU] was one of the best things that could have ever happened to me at [King High School], to be perfectly honest ... It was a really great experience and um, it teaches you know, young Black men and women more about themselves and how to, you know, love yourselves and love your hair and your skin. (Nia, Interview #2, December 8, 2012)

After reviewing my interviews with former members, and analyzing the remaining data sources, it was clear that Black Girls United was a key actor in several participants' heightened self-confidence. Yet, it is critical to acknowledge that the program did not equally influence the learners. For some individuals, the Black feminist pedagogy simply ignited "a little spark" (Kenya, Interview #2, December 12, 2013). However, other students insisted that Black Girls United was "one of the best things that could have happened" during high school (Nia, Interview #2, December 8, 2012). Notwithstanding the variance in degrees of impact, the general rise in BGU members' self-confidence resulted in diverse acts of oppositional resistance.

Several Black Girls United members recalled engaging in strategic efforts to operate *outside* of the box of traditional Black femininity. Tanya, a former student, insisted that her involvement in BGU calmed her intimidation in social settings—which was a product of society's deficit views of urban Black girls. In fact, she drew on her marginalization as an impetus to achieve "the unexpected" (Tanya, Interview #2, December 22, 2012). In my conversation with Tanya, she stated:

> It helped me learn how to be strong. Like this is what I want, this is how I feel, and I don't care what *anyone* has to say. And I don't care how society views me, and that's just what it is! Before [BGU], I really wasn't like that. Like you know, it was like, "Well I *wanna* do this, and I *wanna* do that," but that was it. *And I felt intimidated* and I felt like, "Hmmm, that's not something I should be doing as a *woman*," or "Maybe that's not something I should doing because I was *Black*," [BGU] was there and it helped me reconfigure that whole train of thinking. And I felt like, "Nah, I *can* do that. I *should* do that. Matter of fact, I *better* do that. Just because they say I *can't* do that, now I really want to accomplish it!" You know, like, I just wanted to be *great*. (Tanya, Interview #2, December 22, 2012)

According to Tanya—as well as several additional BGU members—it was necessary to strive for overall greatness and surpass society's limited scope of African American girls' social possibilities. One stereotype that numerous students challenged was Black women's alleged sexual immorality. By far, the most-examined issue in BGU was the omnipresent, controlling representation of young African American women in popular youth cultural media, as sex-obsessed, modern day Jezebels (Morgan, 1999). We often contemplated this phenomenon at random, even when the initial topic on the agenda was starkly different.

For instance, during our twenty-second week of class, the learners were entrenched in a conversation about Assata Shakur and Angela Davis's journeys as political prisoners (BGU class, Week 42). Remarkably, students transitioned from a discussion about the inhumane treatment of African American young and adult women revolutionaries in U.S. prisons, to debating the consequences of Black women's tacit participation in their sexual objectification. After significant banter about how teenagers often mimic the lewd dance moves that are at the center of contemporary music videos, several individuals admitted using greater discretion at school dances because of their involvement in BGU.

Andrea:	After reading, and this stuff [looking at a stack of previous readings on her desk] and what we be talkin' about in here, I don't even mess with a lot of those songs. Like, I just go outside and cool off. Come back when the music's not so bad.
Chloe:	What? Then I guess you ain't *never* dancin', [laughing] 'cuz it's *always* bad. That's why I just don't go anymore. I'm good. I rather stay home and eat takeout.
Andrea:	Ain't no takeout comin' to yo' neighborhood! [Laughing] I'm just kiddin'. But foreal, you know what I mean. Some of it's worse.
Ashanti:	I ain't never seen [Chloe] go outside to cool off! [Class laughs] Naw, but I feel you. Like, … and I can't even say that I don't dance to [disrespectful music], 'cuz I do. Sometimes. Probably most of the time. It's the *way* you dance tho. You ain't gotta dance like a hooker. I ain't finna be lookin like a *tramp* out here in these streets. Especially cuz' everybody know I be in here wit ya'll *every week*. Like, I don't want *nobody* seeing me act a fool and be like, "Ain't she a [BGU student]? Ain't she in [BGU]?"
Tanisha:	And you *know* you gon' get called out too! Somebody'll see you and tell Ms. Lane! *Huh, Ms. Lane?*
Ms. Lane:	I have eyes and ears all over this school! [Looks around the class with a stern expression.]
Chloe:	*See*?! That's why I don't even go man! [Class laughs] Naw I'm just kidding. I just don't want people lookin' at me like that *period*. And … I used to *really* think that was cute. Like really thought it was … like, I was big shit dancing to those songs. Trying to fit in. But … now, *I'm good*! As much as we talk about how degrading it is up in here, *I'm good*. Foreal.
Ashanti:	But, I feel like, I'm not gon' be influenced by *other* people. Like, even *outside* of them dances. I'm not following *nobody*. And *not*

just cuz' I be like, "Oh, Ms. Lane gon' find out." Because a lot of like, like I remember certain situations that happened, and like outside of [BGU], and I'm with my friends and some bull-shit happens, and I'm just like "Yeah, nah I'm cool." Like I'll *really* look at it from *our* perspective. How we would look at something in [BGU] versus just how I be out with my friends. I be like, "No y'all look like *rats*. I'm bout to *go*. Like fo' real, fo' real." Especially like with *my* lil crew. Like, they *really* out there. Sometimes I have to really—just have to step back and be like, "Aye, y'all doin' too much. I'm bout to go. *Take me home*." Cause I could end up like a lot of them. Like, a lot of girls that's havin' sex in bathrooms and all kind of stuff, cuz' TV says that's what you have to do to get liked by boys at school. That really ain't my cup of tea. I'm *cool* on that.

The conversation between Andrea, Chloe, and Ashanti demon-strates how the young women developed new perspectives about their individual and collective displays of sexuality and the connotations of sexual openness. This paradigm shift, in large part, was influenced by the weekly discourse in Black Girls United. Through multiple exchanges among BGU peers, numerous individuals recognized that fictive nar-ratives about Black women's bodies—in the media and through other social discourses—was fundamental to their subjectivity as urban ado-lescents. In addition to altering their behavior by choosing to refrain from perceived "lewd activities" (Chloe, BGU class, Week 42), the par-ticipants in BGU were also *vocal* in their resistance against repressive cultural politics and social misrepresentations.

Holla if You Hear Me!: Coming to Voice in BGU

The findings of this research suggest that Black Girls United inspired numerous members to utilize their power to confront the social alien-ation and political exclusion that African American women and girls have historically endured. hooks (1994) highlights the process of *com-ing to voice*—or speaking without inhibition to end domination—as integral to multiply oppressed groups' revolutionary struggle to be seen, heard, and valued as human beings. Several members of BGU stated that finding their voice, and using it as a gesture of resistance, helped individuals navigate unfair treatment at King High and in their personal lives. In my interview with Ashanti, she discussed how her participation in BGU led her to be more assertive in her communication with her mother:

> I became *way* more vocal. And expressing—like, really just expressing myself like to *anybody*. Any and *everybody*. Like my mom catches it the most I think its cuz I held back for so many years. When I felt she was doin' wrong. I would just, like, not say nuthin'. Like I, I just, I'd just cry or like I said, I'd write. Like a lot of times I used to cry. Nobody knew I was a *big ass cry baby* [laughing], but I would just go in the room and be like— cry, cry, cry, cry, come out smiling, and nobody'll ever know. Like, regardless of how she would take it, regardless of how she would feel, like since [BGU], I'm just like hella—when it come to expressing myself, whatever's on my chest, I'm bout to *say it*! And I think that [BGU] like helped me with that. Like *a lot*. Cuz' at first I wouldn't talk about nuthin'. Like you couldn't get me to talk. Even in class and stuff. I was just quiet before. Now I be like—always got sumthin' to say. People probably be wantin' me to just *shut up*! (Ashanti, Interview #2, December 1, 2012)

Ashanti was typically reserved before joining Black Girls United. Yet after two years of participating in the program, she no longer feared other people's reactions to her self-expression. As a product of her heightened self-confidence, Ashanti bravely exposed her anger, fear, pain, and vulnerability to other individuals—particularly her peers at King High School, and her mother.

Similarly, Nia's process of *coming to voice* involved unveiling her opinions and emotions more liberally. Nia was particularly enraged and outspoken when young men students at King High School used epithets, such as the term "bitch," to reference young African American women students. In our second interview (Nia, Interview #2, December 8, 2012), she recalled pledging for a moratorium on the term:

Nia: And I remember talking to a boy or whatever—wow, that's funny I just remembered that—and he was like "Where you goin'?" And I'm like "I'm going to my [BGU] meeting." He's like, and excuse the word, he was like "That's where the *smart bitches* go to huh?" [Laughing]. That's funny I just remembered that. I was like, "Why would you call your Black friend a *bitch*? How are we bitches?" He was like, "In a good way." I said, "A bitch is *never* good!" Like damn, I started going straight *preacher* on him. I was like, "Would you refer to your *mom* as

Interviewer: a bitch, in the *good* way?" And he was just like "Alright, that's where the *smart* girls go." You know, like—and I noticed outside, people were like, oh those are, those are the smart girls. Those are those girls who, you know, those girls want more in life [laughing].

Interviewer: And your decision to speak up was somehow connected to your participation in the program?

Nia: Oh yeah! Because, I mean, I know that I found myself because of [BGU]. Like, being able to speak up. Because I hung around a lot of guys, and I was on a mission to end the "b" word and take it off the face of the planet! And what I noticed was that around me, it wasn't used. They were like "We're not gonna' even say that word around [Nia] because we know we're gonna' be hearing the, hearing the—"

Interviewer: [Interrupting] Hearing the *sermon* today!

Nia: Yeah, like, "She about to go hard on us for the b-word!" So around me … so around me, I started noticing different things. Like certain people who would act a certain way that I wasn't cool with—I started noticing like that's *not* what I'm about. Like, we can be cool but I don't have to accept that behavior in my inner circle, just because that's how you are and because we wanna' be friends. You know, *I can't*. And I'm *gonna'* speak up about it. I'm not comfortable with that, and I'm not havin' it, and that's *just it*.

In sum, the four elements of my Black feminist pedagogical framework (i.e., *critical feminist literature, positioning students as change agents, a politicized ethic of care,* and *collectivity*) ignited a flame in students that inspired them to create empowered identities. Additionally, as numerous Black girl learners' self-confidence amplified, individuals' used their *voice* to fight daily attacks on their individual and collective humanity.

A More Positive Orientation Towards School

The initial aim of this study was to explore the effects of Black feminist pedagogy on BGU members' race and gender identities. Moreover, I was eager to investigate whether my Black feminist pedagogy assisted students in navigating the social and academic barriers at King High School. The previous section examines how BGU students' processes of *coming to voice* inspired individuals to defy demeaning stereotypes about

Black women and girls—especially during social interactions at King (e.g., school dances and peer-to-peer communications). Interestingly, the data also suggests that the learners' participation in Black Girls United generally resulted in more positive educative outlooks.

Chapter Four revealed that several BGU participants had an unenthusiastic outlook towards school and were academically disengaged before their membership in the organization. Students' heightened feelings of *invisibility* and *hypervisibility* materialized from the social and academic barriers that Black girl learners typically encountered inside and outside of the educational context. An analysis of the data unmasked three specific ways that my Black feminist pedagogy prompted a shift in participants' orientations towards school. Students' *intellectual dispositions,* and *purposes* for and desire to attend school shifted as a result of their membership in the program.

Intellectual Empowerment in BGU

Approximately one semester after the inception of Black Girls United, the young women in Black Girls United had garnered a distinct reputation at King High School. Students perceived BGU participants as "smart" and "wanting more in life" than the typical urban adolescent (Tanisha, BGU class, Week #12). Black Girls United was a reservoir of social *and* intellectual stimulation, which distinguished the organization from other extra-curricular activities that African American girl students archetypally joined, such as cheerleading and extramural sports. Numerous learners maintained that there was an "unspoken, queen-like culture" in BGU that inspired individuals to "be smarter overall" (Lisa, BGU class, Week #53). In my second interview with Lisa, she articulated this belief with fervor:

> We created like this, this *queen-like culture,* where it's like, "You're a queen … this is what you are, you are not gonna' act like anything less than that. You're gonna go to class, you gonna get your butt in there on time, you gonna do your work" and it's like, it was a—I guess I can say for me, *it was a unspoken requirement.* It was just like, "Ok well, no one ever told me that this how you're going to act in [BGU], or this is how we want you to respond and things like that," but it was just, "Ok well, now that you've decided that this club is

something that you want to participate in, and now that we have this, now that we've embraced each other as sisters, we're gonna uphold each other to this standard."(Lisa, Interview #2, January 4, 2013)

Intellectual empowerment was a significant benefit of participating in Black Girls United. Similar to other learners, Lisa believed that "being smart" was an unspoken rule in BGU—which was a surprising finding.

As the faculty sponsor of the program, I did not require members to maintain a certain grade point average or academic standing. In fact, Black girl learners' intellectual proclivity flowered due to the influence of their *peers*. Nia recalled:

> When I came to [BGU] it was like, "This is home. This is where I can express myself. This is where I can learn." I could finally voice my opinion and formulate educated discussions. We learned *so many* different things. And when I say I knew it all, I thought nobody could teach me *anything*, because of what we were being taught [in BGU]. *I* was *challenged*. Listening to everybody else, and how they would speak made me want to *get my dictionary swag*! [Laughing] Like, I felt—how some people used to speak—I was like, "Hold on! I don't know about this! You're using a bigger word! I don't even know what that word means!" And I started feeling, like, *inferior* and I was like "Okay, I'm gonna' have to get my dictionary swag. You know, I'm gonna' have to change the way I say certain things. I'm gonna' have to fix the way I speak out loud." It's like everybody had stepped up their game. It just made me want to be smarter. (Nia, Interview #2, December 8, 2012)

In my second interview with Nia, she disclosed that her membership in Black Girls United inspired her to become a stronger intellectual. Her peers' expansive vocabularies motivated Nia to improve her mental Rolodex of "bigger word[s]" (Nia, Interview #2, December 8, 2012). Furthermore, before joining the program, Nia associated intelligence with *whiteness*. She admitted, "I used to want to be the little Jewish white girl, who is smart and rich and has a maid." Conversely, after one semester in Black Girls United, Nia was "proud to be an African American young woman," and realized that "being a Black girl and being intelligent go hand in hand; it's not an *unusual* thing!" (Nia, Interview #2, December 8, 2012).

In several of the videotaped Black Girls United meetings, I discovered that the participants often made references to "feeling smarter" (Danielle, BGU class, Week #19) when they were amongst their BGU peers. Additionally, individuals often asserted that their opinions about intelligence had changed as a result of the program. Prior to joining BGU, several learners believed that smart, urban Black girls were anomalies—which is similar to what Nia reported during her interview. However, after experiencing the Black feminist pedagogy in BGU, numerous members dramatically altered their stance, and *expected* every participant to be "smarter than average" (Erykah, BGU class, Week #38) and work more diligently in their classes.

In the following transcript from meeting #60 (out of a total of 72 sessions), three students—Tanya, Daniella, and Chrisette—explain how their hankering for academic excellence materialized during their tenure in the program.

Tanya: When people ask me, when they ask me what I do in here, and like, I'm like, "I'm Vice President," then they automatically have a expectation that I'm like a straight A student. [Laughing] *Which ain't the truth!* But like, so, it's pressure, like I don't know how people think that—

Chloe: [Interrupting] I think it's cuz' we in the magnet too. You know—

Tanya: [Interrupting] But I don't know if it's that because it's a lot of girls in the magnet. Like, a *gang* of Black girls in the magnet, and they not focused in school.

Andrea: And everybody in here ain't in the magnet.

Tanya: You right. So … honestly, like, the *magnet* thing. I don't think that's the case.

Daniella: It's because we walkin' around with a big ass *QUEEN* on our shirts! You ever met a *stupid* queen? I haven't! [Laughing] Like, if you're a queen, you're … you're above everyone. Except Kings, or, I guess … . But, like, if you a queen you have a higher standard. We *have* to be smart. We *have* to try harder. We *have* to set a example. Even if you didn't think you was coming here for that—I know I wasn't even thinkin' like that at first. I was just like, I'm gonna' see what this program is about, and I liked it, but I wasn't thinking about really setting no example. But then, after some weeks I was like, wearing the shirt, and we always reading about important stuff in here, so I was like, "Yeah, I gotta improve. I gotta set a example." We about more than the regular—"Oh she think she cute. She in cheer. She play ball." Like, we gotta be on point with our grades and stuff.

Chrisette
(facilitator):   Ok wait, who else felt like they had to do better to be in [BGU]? I did, cuz' I was like I'm not about to *embarrass myself*. Everybody came to—to *work*, it seem like. On the first day! I was like, man! I gotta come correct. Even in my other classes. Cuz like, like [Daniella] said, [BGU girls] are *supposed* to be smarter. That's how you looked at. And the teachers too. [Ms. Ross] always winkin' at me when I wear my shirt. Like—she's proud. And it makes me try harder, and be smarter because people expect us to do good and set a good example. We from [BGU], like, we [*BGU girls*]!

Tanya: Well I don't know about ya'll cuz my grades were already good when I started! [Laughing] No, but forreal, it did make me smarter and made me wanna', like, *try harder* cuz people watchin' us, forreal. And on top of that, like, before we read all this stuff I used to—I had read about "Oh this dude invented this, or oh this other Black dude fought this war," but like, where were the women? How did we make history? And like, [BGU], in [BGU] everything is about women and it's like, you know what? *We're smart too! I am somebody!* Ya'll was just hiding it from us! So it tells me that—like I said—people think I'm supposed to be smart, and that's good cuz' people thinkin' that's, like—it's a *white thing* to be smart and get good grades. But I'm like, "Sorry, you're *wrong*. It is a *Black* thing. And not just for the men. [Black young women] too!"

According to the Black Girls United participants, King High school teachers and non-BGU affiliated peers' *expectations* sparked immense pressure for BGU members to embody academic giftedness. Additionally, wearing the red *Queen* shirts each week played an essential role in students' decisions to work harder in their classes, and their efforts to set a "good example" for other African American young women at King (Chrisette, BGU class, Week #60). Reflecting on her days as a high school student, Nia recalled that "folks were looking at [BGU girls] regardless, so [the members] figured they might as well be inspiring." Thus, for many participants, a newfound *purpose* for attaining an education triggered their longing for intellectual and academic growth. Self-edification *and* community uplift became the impetus behind students' educational pursuits.

Education for Liberation: Shifts in the Purpose of Schooling

For urban African American girls, school can be a mercurial reality, of sorts. These spaces are often unpredictable and volatile in nature—which is an especially challenging environment for intersectionally minoritized populations to navigate. Fittingly, before Black Girls United, it was difficult for the learners to steer themselves with certainty about their academic aspirations and life outcomes. However, after engaging with my Black feminist pedagogical framework (*critical feminist literature, positioning students as change agents,* a *politicized ethic of care,* and *collectivity*), BGU learners' perspectives about their educational goals and purposes expanded. In the early weeks of the program (i.e., weeks 1 through 5), we drew on African American philosophies of education, which stress sacrifice, service, and community liberation (Perry, Steele, & Hilliard 2003). This conceptual frame became the backdrop of frequent subsequent conversations about the girls' educational pursuits. Participants were also inspired by the National Association of Colored Women's (NACW) adage, *lifting as we climb.* It is, therefore, befitting that various data revealed how students adopted the expression as an ideological mantra. In the following example, Brittany discussed how the impetus behind her desire to achieve a high level of formal education shifted considerably:

> I realized that the more you learn, the better you are for yourself. And then you can *share that* with others. I came in knowing that education is important because my parents were big on that. Not going to college and getting my degree wasn't an option. *Not for me!* I knew, like "You don't have to be like everyone else—hanging out, having kids." [Laughs] Partying—like, you *can,* but there's better things you can be doing. And that's the biggest thing I advocate for. You know, but to add to that—and I learned this from [the program], even with like my cousins and everyone younger than me, whatever you wanna do, make sure you have options. You have to have options. Don't limit yourself. And going to school provides you with options. Furthering any education, in any field, it gives you options. It gives you the *tools.* And you *can* be an example! The biggest thing—what's most important—is, you know, you can do better for *yourself,* for your *family,* and for your *community.* All three. And that was the biggest lesson for me. What's the point of it all, if you're not helping other's—other *people* along the way? (Brittney, Interview #1, October 19, 2012).

Before joining Black Girls United, education was a top priority for Brittney, and her parents regularly reinforced the importance of being a high achiever. However, one of the greatest lessons that she acquired as a result of her participation in BGU, was to uplift *other* people on her journey to success. Hence, Brittney's evolved ambitions included learning as much as possible to acquire the "tools" to uplift her family and community in her quest for personal development (Brittney, Interview #1, October 19, 2012). Likewise, in my interview with Lisa, another former member, she stressed why it was imperative to set a positive example for her family and community members. However, for Lisa, her younger and impressionable sister was her motivation for attaining educational success:

> Lisa: My drive has been my baby sister. Once I realized that it was ok to *be* intelligent. That I should be proud of that. Like, *you* showed me that. We used to talk about it—like, it's something to be proud of, you know? And I wanted to be a trendsetter at [King]. Like, once I realized that, it was like, I got do good for my little sister too.
>
> Interviewer: How old is she?
>
> Lisa: Well, she's— now she is 14. So, um, yea, like, I wanted her to know that she can make it and I mean, my mom, she has seven kids. *Seven* of us, and everybody knows the statistics. Foster kids, you got *seven* of them and out of all of us that are adults, I'm the *only one* that made it. And one out of seven of us, you know, its not … it's not …
>
> Interviewer: Yea, poor statistics
>
> Lisa: You know it's not really too good. So um, she's been my drive for a very long time and just showing her like oh okay I do the things that I do because I want you to see the things—something *better* than what you always see, or what you've been seeing your entire life. *I tell her today, I don't care what you do, I want you to strive to be better than what I am.* So with her seeing me doing something and me using her as my drive all these years, and just allowing her to see something different, it allows me to keep pushing.

During my individual interviews with Brittney and Lisa, I discovered that after only one semester of participating in Black Girls United, both young women's commitment to enhancing their family and community members' lives deepened. Alternatively, other BGU learners experienced a similar ideological shift much later in the program. For instance, an eleventh-grader named Daniella had a moment of revelation and insight about "giving back," which occurred near the end of the program.

On the day of our final BGU meeting (Week #70), I discovered a small greeting card in my mailbox from Daniella that was accompanied by a written note expressing her gratitude for my labors as the faculty sponsor. To conclude, she added:

> I want to be like you when I get older. At first I didn't realize these things, but after all of your college degrees I'm happy to see a Black person can still be dedicated to the community and want to be here with us. You want to see us improve, and that is what I would like to do when I finish college and become a teacher. (Daniella, Alternate correspondence, Week #69)

In sum, the young women in Black Girls United learned to value school beyond its function as a means of employability. Although the students unearthed varied and diverse reasons for pursuing an education, they experienced a collective paradigm shift that resulted from the radical messaging in BGU about self *and* community liberation.

Together, the learners' intellectual empowerment—and their altered consciousness regarding the *purpose* of school—was accompanied by a greater *desire* to show up regularly. In my discussions with numerous Black Girls United members, most students alleged that school was dreadfully uneventful. Moreover, a handful of participants believed that attending King High was a "waste of time" altogether (Tanisha, BGU class, Week #3). Thus, for several members, BGU was an exciting place of refuge that liberated African American young women's latent joy through intellectual stimulation and social and cultural validation. The learners often cited the spirit of *collectivity* as the primary source of their sustained engagement in the program. In my interview with Erykah, she maintained that her Black Girls United "sisters's" intellectual prowess was a tremendous source of inspiration and the reason why she "never missed school on a Thursday" (Erykah, Interview #2, January 19, 2013). Mainly enthused by the juniors and seniors, Erykah noted:

[BGU] motivated me when I didn't feel like coming to school. I loved the conversations and the sisterhood. *Especially* [Andrea]. She was just always like in there, like, "No, men should do this. Us women, you know, we gotta do this, we gotta do that." And I always would look at her, I'm like *wow*. I was like, "I hope I become that outspoken one day." Yeah, I loved hearing everybody speak. Especially the older girls, and [Andrea] because she always told it how it was. It made me more confident. Like, as a little sister—a young *Queen*—I had someone to look up to, and I knew that on Thursdays I was gonna' come to school and *learn something*, and *actually* have fun. (Erykah, Interview #2, January 19, 2013)

The *collectivity* that emerged in Black Girls United opposed the custom of competition among girl adolescents, which was primarily detrimental to King High School girls' social relationships and psychological well-being. In my first round of individual interviews with former BGU learners, the students unanimously agreed that the African American girls at King High were infamous for "bring[ing] the drama" (Brittney, Interview #1, October 9, 2012). As such, the BGU members' involvement in a culture that promoted *sisterhood* and *oneness* was a welcomed form of resistance—and an audacious embrace of the unknown.

In 35 hours of video transcripts, I counted 326 occasions in which students directly and explicitly referred to themselves or their peers as a "*Queen*." On 75 separate occasions, one or more students candidly referred to me as a "*Queen*" during class. Although its use is often debated among urban popular culture critics, in the context of BGU, the Black girl learners used the term *Queen* to empower, uplift, and as a proclamation of love and appreciation. The terminology was, therefore, one of the highest compliments that a young woman could receive, and was evidence of the members' efforts to re-define and express themselves on their own terms. Foluke, a former BGU participant, remarked, "If a person is considered to be a *Queen*, that means that they are beautiful, smart, powerful, and highly respected" (Foluke, BGU class, Week #56). In light of these findings, it is no surprise that the BGU participants reported an increase in their *desire* to attend school during their membership in the program.

Conclusion: Meeting Once a Week
"Ain't Hardly Enough"

During my tenure as the sponsor of Black Girls United, I often found myself reciting an old English proverb to my King High School colleagues. Like a record on repeat, I'd cheerily say, "Necessity is the mother of invention!" I was moved to share this adage when my peers inquired about the origins of BGU. A vast majority of the faculty were misinformed and surmised that I had developed the program to remedy African American girl adolescents' problematic and pathological behaviors. In response to the rhetoric, I'd retort that Black Girls United was not a genius ploy to "fix" Black girl learners—whom they deemed as *troubled* and *at-risk*. Rather, the organization was a creative endeavor that originated from the necessity to arm Black girls against social shaming, vicious attacks on their fragile identities, and other school-related threats to their personhood.

Indeed, Black Girls United was a consciousness-raising, counter-cultural phenomenon at King High School. In my interactions with BGU youth, the learners revealed how constant negotiations of their perceived *invisibility* and *hypervisibility* at King High siphoned their love of learning and self-confidence. Before joining the program, several individuals engaged in harmful behaviors, such as ditching school or class, excessive tardiness, and underperformance in core academic subject areas. The findings of this inquiry indicate that my Black feminist pedagogical framework (i.e., *critical feminist literature, positioning students as change agents, a politicized ethic of care,* and *collectivity*) gave students the tools to struggle against the all-consuming primacy of their alienation. Previous sections have illuminated how the organization enabled the participants' purposeful evolution—a practice that I call *#BlackGirlJoy*. Black Girls United members' #BlackGirlJoy took shape in three specific ways: (a) the learners' heightened critical consciousness of African American women's socio-political location, (b) an empowered sense of self that rejected popular notions of Black femininity, and (c) a more positive orientation towards school.

Notwithstanding the unmistakable success of the program, my analysis of the interview data concluded with a sobering revelation. My

conversations with Ashanti exposed how BGU did not sufficiently supply her with the ideological capital to subvert threats to her humanity
over a *sustained* period. Ashanti's social and intellectual empowerment
was limited to our class time, as she regressed to self-defeating behaviors and beliefs immediately following the weekly meetings:

Ashanti: It's kind of hard because it's like you learn so much in thirty
minutes and then you go right back out, and everything go in
one ear and out the other. Like it wasn't enough time to *grasp*
everything. But you know, it's crazy how much those thirty
minutes, once a week can open your eyes too! But then, it's like,
you go out and try to face all that shit and try to keep everything that you had in them thirty minutes in yo' head. And at
the end of the day you just like, *it's hard*. Especially as a teenager. Like, I don't know. It get's hard. Cause you wanna'—you
don't want to look like—you kind of want to be that person
that everybody likes. A lot of people want to be like that, but
you gotta get it in yo'self and be comfortable with yourself to
where you don't fall into the trap. Where you can be smarter,
and think twice about shit. Like, look deeper. I think that's
what I had to do a lot too.

Interviewer: Hmmm … can you give me an example?

Ashanti: I can remember situations like we would talk about somethin'
in class like, "Damn! Like that's crazy." And then I'll go to a
party and like do like the *total opposite* of what we just talked
about! Of what we all said we would stop doin'! It's like it would
go in one ear—and when you there, you really see everything
clear. Because it was like that lunch was thirty minutes, right.
It's impacting you when you sittin' inside of the classroom and
you really talking about it, and you analyzing the world and
like everything that's going on. But then it's like—okay, lunchtime is over. Friday comes. Now it's the weekend. You out with
all yo' homies, you not thinking about nothing you talked about
at lunchtime on Thursday! So it's like, even if [BGU] was longer,
I think it would've had to be *way* more sessions of it to make a
bigger difference.

Interviewer: Ok, now I understand how it didn't give you the tools you
needed to make huge or, maybe lasting changes in your behavior, socially. Right? But what about school? Like, *academically*?
Do you recall any changes in that area of your life?

Ashanti: Well, in the first year, of [BGU] yeah. I was doin' real good,
cuz' you was my English teacher too. But after that—in my 12th
grade year—*not really*, cuz' … well, I think it *could* have. But I

never came across another teacher like you, so after I left your 11th grade honors English class and I went to uh, this other AP English class. He taught *completely* different! So it was really like, I went *right back* to how I was before. Like *fo'real, fo'real.* Like I *never* came my 12th grade. My 12th grade year was like a, I wouldn't say a breeze. I wouldn't say a breeze *necessarily,* but yeah … . I felt like my 11th grade year should've been my 12th grade year. Like if I would've left with the *proper knowledge* that I had from 11th grade, *when I had [BGU] and you*—I woulda' been straight. Twelfth grade all I needed was at least one really good—like *really* good teacher like you. Then, if I would've took that [class] 12th grade, it would've been different. But I didn't. Twelfth grade was just [BGU], but—like, then I had all that other time I spent in classes with bad teachers. It was a fucked up situation.

Ashanti's admission speaks volumes about the power of alternative pedagogies when they are simultaneously reinforced in other educational spaces within a school site. As reported earlier in this chapter, and reified by the above transcript—the *combined* effect of my Black feminist pedagogy in Black Girls United, and my frequent displays of authentic caring as Ashanti's English teacher—had a significant, positive impact on her self-assurance, coming to voice, and school engagement. However, because she did not encounter a "really good" teacher in her twelfth-grade year, the unhealthy influences that Ashanti confronted at King High School and in social settings outside of school were more impactful than the brief time that we spent together in BGU.

Overwhelmingly, Black Girls United students believed that their participation in the organization aided school engagement and conceptions of their entangled identities. Still, many members agreed that they would have benefitted from "longer and more frequent meetings" (Kenya, Interview #2, January 12, 2013). For instance, during our second interview, Nia confirmed that she would have "gladly sacrificed more lunches for additional time in the program" (Nia, Interview #2, December 8, 2012). Moreover, she declared that if African American girl learners had access to BGU "on a daily basis," graduation rates would have "skyrocketed" (Nia, Interview #2, December 8, 2012). In sum, my Black feminist pedagogical practice yielded *sustained* #BlackGirlJoy for most students. However, just as weeds stifle the growth of flowers in a garden, structural constraints and deterrents to urban Black girls' development of viable identities are skillfully predatory and omnipresent.

Questions for Deeper Engagement

1. Black Girls United sparked the participants' conscious unfolding—a process that the author calls #*BlackGirlJoy*. How is the concept of #BlackGirlJoy in conversation with the term #BlackGirlMagic? How do both ideas play out in the lives of African American girl-identified youth in your school and community?
2. The outcomes of the Black Girls United program necessitates the need for African American girl adolescents to "be in process" within educational spaces throughout the United States. Black feminist pedagogy, as described in Chapter 4, meets young women where they *are*, and encourages youth to radically dream and hope for what *could be*. Reflect on your pedagogical approach to teaching Black girl learners and other subordinated student populations. How might you center radical visioning and community transformation more intentionally?

Note

1 Patricia Hill Collins characterizes *self-determination* as the "power to decide one's own destiny" (Collins, 2000, p. 300).

References

Bailey, M., & Trudy aka @thetrudz. (2018). On misogynoir: Citation, erasure, and plagiarism. *Feminist Media Studies, 18*(4), 762–768.

Collins, P. (2000). *Black feminist thought: Knowledge, consciousness, and the politics of empowerment* (2nd ed.). New York, NY: Routledge.

Freire, P. (1973). *Pedagogy of the oppressed*. New York, NY: Continuum Press.

Harris-Perry, M. (2011). *Sister citizen: Shame, stereotypes, and Black women in America*. New Haven: Yale University Press.

hooks, b. (1994). *Teaching to transgress: Education as the practice of freedom*. New York, NY: Routledge.

Morgan, J. (1999). *When chickenheads come home to roost: My life as a hip hop feminist*. New York, NY: Simon & Schuster.

Omi, M., & Winant, H. (1994). *Racial formation in the United States: From the 1960s to the 1990s* (2nd ed.). New York, NY: Routledge.

Perry, T., Steele, C., & Hilliard, A. (2003). *Young, gifted and Black: Promoting high achievement among African-American students*. Boston, MA: Beacon Press.

Ross, J. (2020). *Conflicted* (Unpublished manuscript).

Sears, S. D. (2010). *The negotiation of power and identity within the Girls Empowerment Projects*. Albany: SUNY Press.

"I guarantee that the seed you plant in love, no matter how small, will grow into a mighty tree of refuge. We all want a future for ourselves and we must now care enough to create, nurture and secure a future for our children."

~Afeni Shakur

Chapter Seven

Silencing the Ego: Lessons for Developing a Transformative Praxis

As an African American woman researcher who centers Black girl learners, I approached this inquiry with disdain for the myriad social rules—upheld through institutional policies, practices, and discourses—that govern the spaces in African American girl adolescents' educative lives. One outcome of my engagement with this inquiry was an elevated and enriched awareness of the prolonged, intersectional race, class, and gender-based atrocities that young Black women face daily. Previous chapters have drawn on Black Girls United members' narrative qualitative accounts to illumine the egregious misdeeds on African American women and girls in one U.S. public school. In light of these painful realities, *Engendering #BlackGirlJoy* offers a Black feminist pedagogical formula (e.g., *critical feminist literature, positioning students as change agents, a politicized ethic of care,* and *collectivity*) that directly conflicts with ideological and institutional forces that socialize African American young women in urban communities to be silent, accommodating, and non-participative recipients of schooling.

Engaging with innovative curricular strategies and competing narratives of Black femininity elevated BGU participants into lightning rods of *joy*. In Chapter One, I defined #BlackGirlJoy as African American girl learners' *conscious unfolding*—or, the journey to self-define and evolve—in the face of abundant systemic injustices. The members' #BlackGirlJoy manifested in three specific ways. Several students reported: (a) heightened awareness of African American women's socio-political location, (b) an empowered sense of self that rejected popular, reductive notions of Black femininity, and (c) a more positive orientation towards school. Hence, this study enriches the body of research that highlights effective methods of academic instruction that *reconcile* Black girl students' tenacious marginalization.

Education scholars have investigated the utility of Black feminist pedagogy,, specifically as an unorthodox strategy for engaging African American girl adolescents (Henry, 1998, 2009; Mogadime, 2000; Muhammad & Haddix, 2016; Sears, 2010). As an extension of existing literature, I explored how a *holistic* application of Black feminist pedagogy impacts the race and gender identities of African American girl learners in an *urban* context, over an *extended* period, *within* a U.S. public school. Moreover, this study offers new ways of defining, characterizing, and interpreting Black feminist pedagogy. I have demonstrated how the combined four features of my framework had an added influence on how BGU members' race-gender identities and schooling attitudes and behaviors changed over time. The findings chapters illuminated the kinds of discourse that characterized those moments.

Unearthing a pedagogical framework that incites #BlackGirlJoy invites readers to consider the factors that hinder P-12 practitioners as they attempt to cultivate a transformative praxis. As Freire (2002) has noted, traditional education is fashioned to serve a political agenda: teaching young people to receive their education and adapt to the world passively. By contrast, liberating curricula inspires youth to—in their "vocation of becoming more fully human"—engage the world with increasing critical awareness, and become agents of revolutionary change (p. 44). In the following sections, I employ the wisdom of the BGU learners to generate a set of takeaways that practitioners can ponder to achieve these ambitious, yet attainable, outcomes. Centralizing the members' voices empowers Black girl adolescents in the process of democratizing education for countless African American girls—and other vulnerable student populations—who will boldly follow in their footsteps.

A Slice of Humble Pie: Reflections on My Black Feminist Pedagogical Past

Historically, African American women practitioners have employed Black feminist pedagogy to harness subordinated youth's oppositional knowledge construction as a bridge to self-discovery and community empowerment. Moreover, a common aim among these educators is to help learners navigate schooling with their humanity, integrity, and cultural knowledge intact (Joseph, 1995; Mogadime, 2000). While Black women practitioners are often embroiled in the day-to-day chaos of teaching in challenging social and institutional settings, upholding the aforementioned ideals calls for us to intentionally re-examine our praxis. Reflecting on our ideological postures and curricular choices may inspire an upending of outdated approaches and the development of frameworks that are dynamic and responsive to today's youth.

While conducting this study, I often contemplated why my implementation of Black Feminist pedagogy was successful in Black Girls United—yet, it was marginally effective according to the African American girl learners in my conventional English classes. An analysis of the data and the collective viewpoints of the BGU participants revealed the limitations of my prior practice: I did not apply the elements of my Black feminist pedagogical framework *consistently, holistically*, and *authentically*.

For instance, my English students seldom engaged with *critical feminist literature*. The majority of the assigned readings—which the school district strongly encouraged—centered the perspectives of White men, and only occasionally persons of color. Moreover, these written works rarely measured up to the trifecta for intellectually stimulating curricula: cultural relevance, present-day applicability, *and* captivating content. Black Girls United students alleged that the *simultaneity* of these three features in *each* literary source was fundamental to the participants' motivation to complete the weekly readings.

Moreover, I learned that the strict organizational structure and policies of my classroom did not *position students as change agents*. As a second-year teacher in my early twenties, I was hyper-vigilant about meeting district-mandated benchmarks for student performance on standardized assessments. Consequently, my focus was to maintain order and adhere to old-fashioned notions of rigor, which garnered praise from the school administration. As the instructor of my classes, I had the option to be more flexible. Still, I maintained an unyielding program of study (e.g., assigned readings, and the length and frequency of homework assignments and quizzes). In my traditional classes, I planned *for* students, not *alongside* youth. This strategy limited learners' opportunities to exercise their autonomy and leadership capabilities, which was in direct contrast to the structure of Black Girls United and other liberatory paradigms.

Working in a school with large class sizes also posed a threat to the third element of my Black feminist pedagogical framework: *a politicized ethic of care*. As a self-identified feminist and social justice educator, I had an authentic concern with students' social and educative development beyond the bounds of my classroom. However, I was responsible for teaching approximately 150 students, which severely restricted my ability to connect with individuals on a deeper, personal level. Regretfully, I did not cultivate close and lasting relationships with a majority of my young Black women English students as I did with the small group of BGU youth. Hence, my embodiment of care was fatigued, and the young African American women in my traditional classes may have regarded my efforts as insincere and inadequate.

Finally, we typically established *collectivity* in my English classes during community-building activities (e.g., performance poetry) that took place at the beginning of the school year. Such short-lived displays of commiseration and solidarity failed to produce enduring, mutually supportive rapports between students. Moreover, I often encouraged young people to compete for grades during tests and quizzes— individually, or during small group activities. Accordingly, the spirit of competition that I unconsciously manufactured in my general English classes worked against my ambition to unite students as allies.

To conclude, it is crucial for practitioners to make pedagogical pivots when our methods don't live up to our aspirations. This is especially necessary for educators who teach African American girl learners—considering the traditional curricula's flattening force on these students' social and academic development. Additionally, pre- and in-service educators who wish to utilize the Black feminist pedagogical framework outlined in this inquiry should proceed cautiously. According to the members of Black Girls United, the key to applying these methods effectively is employing the four elements of the pedagogy *consistently, holistically,* and *authentically.* A superficial approach stifles the potential for African American young women to unite in solidarity, as autonomous leaders and engaged scholars.

Three Key Takeaways from Urban Girl Learners

Practitioners who operate with fanatic allegiance to *played-out* curricular paradigms are widespread in U.S. schools. Evading a "praxis of domination" and facilitating transformative learning calls for an educator to yield to the wisdom of young people (Freire, 2002, p. 126). Bettina Love's (2019) nuanced concept of abolitionist teaching deepens this notion. Among other facets, abolitionist teaching involves "new ways of showing dark children that they are loved in this world" (p. 88). I argue that a) deeply listening to Black girls' perspectives, b) valuing their experiences, and c) taking *action* that is guided by students' insights are fundamental to pedagogical love. As such, the following sections spotlight three recommendations from the young women in Black Girls United. Each point uncovers a powerful lesson that I have carried into my work as a teacher educator. I am hopeful that these principles will enable meaningful reflection among other practitioners who aspire to wield their teaching in the direction of social justice.

#1: Dare to be Innovative

One noteworthy outcome of this research is unearthing our education system's languid approaches to rectifying the discriminations that suppress Black girls' ability to flourish. The jarring counternarratives of the students in Black Girls United have provided new revelations into how urban African American young women's identities are co-constructed and mediated within educational institutions. Moreover, this inquiry has demonstrated the degree to which a Black feminist pedagogical framework positively influences these learners' self-concepts and participation in school.

In light of the #BlackGirlJoy that this inquiry bore into being, it is critical to acknowledge Bartolomé's (1994) directive preemptively. Cautioning practitioners of the dangers of "one size fits all" approaches to developing methods of instruction, the author notes:

> Although it is important to identify useful and promising instructional programs and strategies, it is erroneous to assume that blind replication of instructional programs or teacher mastery of particular teaching methods, in and of themselves, will guarantee successful student learning, especially when we are discussing populations that historically have been mistreated and [mis]educated by the schools. (p. 408)

Hence, an educator must engage in critical examinations of their practice and consider young Black women students' expressed interests and *shifting* cultural sensibilities while implementing innovative curricular strategies. A simple, "copy and paste" approach—one that ignores the subjectivities of African American girl learners in a specific time, social context, and geographic location—will undoubtedly fail.

The BGU members' perspectives are in line with Bartolomé's assertions. During our weekly meetings and in the individual interviews, the young women explained that no formula or single technique could ensure repeated success in classrooms. On several occasions, the participants discussed the importance for teachers to possess stamina, courage, and ingenuity as they try diverse strategies to meet student needs. The following statements from my interviews with Tanya and Erykah capture the members' collective viewpoints:

> So many teachers are scared. But you have to step out of your box and try something new when what you're doing isn't working. Like, it's *not fair* to your students! To me, a good teacher is creative and curious. They come [to

school] ready to give it everything they got! (Tanya, Interview #2, December 22, 2012)

To be honest, what you did in [BGU], another teacher probably couldn't do in the same way because every teacher is different and every student is different. So you take a new teacher and give him your lessons, and he might *still* suck. So, don't be lazy. You have to be thoughtful about anything you teach to [historically subordinated] kids. *Just be thoughtful!* And switch it up until you get it right. (Erykah, Interview #2, January 19, 2013)

According to the students in Black Girls United, creative instructional strategies—including my Black feminist pedagogical framework—should not be viewed as sure-fire panaceas to the widespread marginalization that African American girl learners encounter in public schools throughout the nation. The members' assertions confirm that for new and experienced teachers alike, unimaginative and misaligned curricular practices are a recipe for disaster. Students absorb the benefits *and* consequences of their teachers' pedagogical decisions—which robustly influence young people's schooling dispositions, academic performance, and eventual life outcomes.

#2: Interrogate Your Positionality and Practice What You Preach

In Melissa Harris-Perry's (2012) book, *Sister Citizen: Shame, Stereotypes, and Black Women in America*, she reminds readers that the misrecognition of Black women is inextricably tied to inequitable access to social, political, and economic goods, which hinders African American women's ability to fully participate as American citizens (p. 42). Harris-Perry's assertion provides a space for researchers to consider the ramifications of systematic educational injustices imposed on Black girl adolescents. To note, Black girls' experiences with structural forms of violence within educational settings—including racism, sexism, cultural hegemony, and more—often overlap due to these youth's entangled social identities (Crenshaw, 1991).

This is perhaps best evidenced by the reductive and myopic constructions of Black femininity in popular media and dominant educational discourses. Rhetoric that positions African American girl adolescent learners as welfare queens, irrationally hostile, sexually immoral, and ratchet compromise these students' humanity and are an enduring threat to their budding identities (Love, 2017; Morris, 2007; Sealey-Ruiz, 2007).[1] These controlling and stereotypical images, moreover, also remain etched in the psyches of practitioners and other school personnel whose deficit ideologies about Black women and girls translate into culturally irresponsible and inhumane engagement with these youth.

In my conversations with the Black Girls United members, the young women insisted that pre- and in-service teachers' systematic self-examinations about their power, privilege, and positionality is essential to remedying dehumanizing pedagogical practices. In these moments of intense reflection, educators must be honest about how their biases and pedagogical blindspots intersect with, and likely poses a threat to, the social and academic well-being of their students. As former member Tanisha noted, the explicit interrogation of the "damaging effects of your flaws" will move practitioners along the path of "knowing better and doing better" (Tanisha, BGU class, Week 21).

As the nation painfully endures intense political turbulence and anti-Black, anti-woman rhetoric, today's teachers have a moral responsibility to *model* how to speak and act in solidarity with vulnerable communities. Admittedly, the BGU youth expressed that "practicing what I preached" inside and outside of our weekly meetings invited the learners to trust, learn from, and evolve with me. In my second conversation with Nia, a former Black Girls United participant, she noted:

> I think it was more of the teacher's presence, let's say that. It was more of your presence. And the respect. Just a genuine—like, you respected everybody. *Every kid*. Even the ones that people called losers. [Laughing] You know? Your classroom was comfortable for those kids too. Even outside of [BGU], your classroom was comfortable. I mean being that you were Ms. Lane, everybody called your classroom home and you opened up your classroom as somewhere to come to—but you're not gonna act a fool! You're going to come here and, I can't even put my finger on it. It was like *you set the tone*. You were positive. You gave us respect and we gave it back to you—and then we gave it to each other. (Nia, Interview #2, December 8, 2012)

Nia proclaimed that "practicing what I preached" was critical to developing and sustaining the positive, affirming energy that she experienced in the program. She noted how teachers often set the tone for how young people behave. Although Black Girls United was a student-centered organization, my "presence" often dictated how the participants interacted. When I interviewed Tanya, another former member, she added that BGU was successful because I "actually represented all of the things that [the organization] stood for" (Tanya, Interview #2, December 22, 2012). Hence, I personified the mission of the program—which, according to Tanya— was "empowering yourself and others." In sum, the Black Girls United learners taught me a valuable lesson: a young person's gaze is analytical, critical, and unflinching. As practitioners, we must *authentically* commit as advocates for the well-being and dignity of all children and embody the principles that we purport to believe.

#3: 'Get Schooled' about Black Girls

As former first lady Michelle Obama articulated in her memoir *Becoming*, "We live by the paradigms we know" (p. 204). Regrettably, the philosophies that undergird many teachers' practices conflict with Black girl learners' cultural knowledge and threatens the radiance of their humanity in educational settings. During my interviews with a representative research sample of seven former Black Girls United members, I asked, *"What do you want new teachers to know about teaching urban African American girls?"* Collectively, the students' greatest concern was the overwhelming number of practitioners whose warped conceptualizations of Black femininity—and limited knowledge about the impact of racism and white supremacy—reinforced these youth's subordination in schools. As Erykah eloquently stated in our second interview, "An African American young woman already has two strikes against her. She's *Black,* and she's a *female.* The last thing she needs is a teacher that makes her feel like she's less than what she's worth" (Erykah, Interview #2, January 19, 2013). The BGU participants maintained that before an educator steps foot in a classroom, they should *do their homework.*

To appreciate the value of Black girl learners, teachers must critically reshape their understandings of Black women's historical and contemporary struggles, and complex social evolution. When I interviewed Kenya, she passionately replied:

> You need to know how we started. Know that we're the *original* women of civilization ... How did we get to where we are today? Don't believe everything you see on TV! *Do your homework*! Know who you're teachin'. And that goes for everybody. Even if you—even if you are a Black woman teacher, or if you're from the hood too. Cuz', just because we're from the same place or we look the same doesn't mean that you've been schooled properly. You know? So, they need to do *their* homework. That way, the process can go smoothly. And you will respect us, and we will trust you, and we will want to learn [from you]. (Kenya, Interview #2, January 12, 2013)

In the quote above, Kenya confirms what educational researchers have long established: race-class and race-gender sameness do not inherently result in humanizing classrooms (Sears, 2010). In my conversations with former Black Girls United participants, individuals credited the success of the program—in large part—to my understanding of their complex realities as urban Black girls. As I noted in earlier chapters, I rooted my initial assumptions about African American young women in unfair generalizations. My previous experience as a young Black woman attending the same high school had tainted my impressions. However, when I failed to engage these youth in my traditional English classes consistently, I learned that a lot had changed. I needed to *get schooled* on African American girls' present-day social location.

As an African American woman and King High School alumnus in my mid-twenties, I had an insider perspective into the lives of my young Black women students as well as the inner workings of the school and surrounding neighborhood. Although I was well-versed in particular community dynamics, six years had passed since I attended King High. Accordingly, the cultural landscape for Black girls had grown increasingly nuanced with the abrasive unfolding of misogyny in popular youth culture. And the depth and variety of social media networking niches, moreover, offered new ways for young people to distribute and consume information (e.g., MySpace, YouTube, Facebook, and Twitter). Thus, I no longer considered myself an expert on how urban African American girls existed in the world.

Harboring a bruised ego, I familiarized myself with the *ever-changing* conditions of young Black women. I became immersed in the local school community (i.e., attending organized sporting and extra-curricular events) and read numerous contemporary texts that my students recommended (i.e., *Confessions of a Video Vixen* by Karrine Steffans and *When Chickenheads Come Home to Roost* by Joan Morgan). Lastly, and perhaps most importantly, I *listened* to my students' diverse stories. I *got schooled* about the modern-day happenings of young Black women, and understood that I could never be a connoisseur of their lives. In short, I had become a lifelong learner. Various data suggests that the BGU members were *most* impressed by my pursuit to understand their experiences more deeply. Investigating students' lived realities—and openly juxtaposing their narratives with mine—enabled the young women to "take off the mask of strength, and be vulnerable" with me (Lisa, Interview #1, November 2, 2012).

Claiming Space for *Sustained* #BlackGirlJoy

In light of the historical ineptitude of education policies, practices, and discourses, this book concludes with an urgent call to action. Collectively, the Black Girls United participants confirmed that in educational contexts where many African American girls are demeaned and alienated on a regular basis, establishing a strong sense of cultural appreciation and self-worth are the *first* steps towards developing more positive schooling behaviors. Furthermore, grounding this inquiry in Black feminist theory (Collins, 2000; hooks, 1989) summons future researchers to frame the schooling experiences of African American girl learners in light of the unique intersecting oppressions they face. As noted by numerous scholars—race, class, gender, and other identity markers are inextricably linked (Morris, 2016; Muhammad & Dixson, 2008). Hence, future examinations of Black youth should continue to center the beautifully multifaceted expressions of their humanity (e.g., bi- or agender, gender non-conforming, LGBTQIA+, nationality/"citizenship status," and learners with disabilities).

At King High School, African American girl learners were incessantly burdened with negotiating narrowly defined social and academic categorizations. Before participating in BGU, numerous members had solitarily endeavored to withstand their subordination. As Brittney Cooper professed in her book *Eloquent Rage* (2018), young Black women are seldom allowed to be *in process* and govern the evolutionary unfolding of their lives. Hence, the Black Girls United program was revolutionary schooling. A grand adventure in self-inquiry, the young scholars dared to interrupt the legacy of cultural genocide in U.S. schools, and in turn, they moved deeper into their authenticity *together*. According to Africa's daughters, #BlackGirlJoy is an ideological refuge and an embodied liberation practice.

The participants of this inquiry have also revealed that sustaining the #BlackGirlJoy that emerged from their collective conversations was difficult in traditional classroom spaces. Before and after our half-hour lunchtime meetings, reductive curricula and vicious rhetoric about Black girlhood invaded these students' psyches. Cooper (2018) contends that *joy* is critical to young women's "ongoing struggle for justice" and their ability to thrive in the world (p. 274). Therefore, I encourage pre- and in-service practitioners—particularly individuals who struggle to engage the intellectual aptitude of African American girl learners—to continue to examine *Black women educators'* pedagogies.

While no singular approach to Black feminist pedagogy exists, much scholarship corroborates Black women teachers' legacy of cultivating triumphant resilience within minoritized student populations. Regretfully, we seldom find Black women's teaching strategies highlighted within discourses of transformative education. Through this research, I hope to strengthen and advance current debates on "academic rigor" and "best practices." Centering and celebrating African American women educators' frameworks is a necessary response to eradicating the marginality that Black *girls specifically* endure in P–12 institutions. Moreover, the rising visibility of exemplary Black women teachers may orient all practitioners toward frameworks that engender anti-oppressive struggle and relentless *joy*.

Questions for Deeper Engagement

1. The Black Girls United scholars targeted three key areas to aid practitioners in cultivating a culturally-sustainable educational praxis: innovation, awareness of oneself as a politicized being, and a *lifelong learner* disposition. Reflect on these recommendations and your current engagement with young people. How do these takeaways show up in your practice? Identify areas for improvement and consider the "next best steps" that you might take to authentically embody these values.

2. The development and ultimate success of Black Girls United can be attributed, in large part, to the author's willingness to engage in critical self-examinations and center student voices as vital resources for enacting change. Reflect on your prior "pedagogical pivots." What inspired you to take new action? Assess how often your learners' wisdom and insights influence your curricular choices?

Note

1 Although the term *ratchet* has various explanations, the epithet is commonly used in popular culture to debase low-income Black women who are deemed loud, hostile, *and* reckless (Love, 2017).

References

Bartolomé, L. I. (1994). Beyond the methods fetish: Toward a humanizing pedagogy. *Harvard Educational Review, 64*(2), 173–195.

Collins, P. H. (2000). *Black feminist thought: Knowledge, consciousness, and the politics of empowerment* (2nd ed.). New York, NY: Routledge.

Crenshaw, K. W. (1991). Mapping the margins: Intersectionality, identity politics, and violence against women of color. *Stanford Law Review, 43*(6), 1241–1299.

Freire, P. (2002). *Pedagogy of the oppressed.* New York, NY: Continuum Press.

Harris-Perry, M. (2011). *Sister citizen: Shame, stereotypes, and Black women in America.* New Haven: Yale University Press.

Henry, A. (1998). "Invisible" and "womanish": Black girls negotiating their lives in an African-centered school in the USA. *Race Ethnicity and Education, 1*(2), 151–170.

Henry, A. (2009). "Speaking up" and "speaking out": Examining "voice" in a reading/writing program with adolescent African Caribbean girls. *Journal of Literacy Research, 30*(2), 233–252.

hooks, b. (1989). *Talking back: Thinking feminist, thinking Black*. Boston, MA: South End Press.

Joseph, G. I. (1995). Black feminist pedagogy and schooling in White capitalist America. In B. Guy-Sheftall (Ed.), *Words of fire: An anthology of African-American feminist thought* (pp. 462–471). New York, NY: The New York Press.

Love, B. (2017). A ratchet lens: Black queer youth, agency, hip hop, and the Black ratchet imagination. *Educational Researcher, 46*(9), 539–547.

Love, B. (2019). *We want to do more than survive: Abolitionist teaching and the pursuit of educational freedom*. Boston, MA: Beacon Press.

Mogadime, D. (2000). Black girls/Black women-centered texts and Black teachers as othermothers. *Journal of the Association for the Research on Mothering, 2*(2), 222–233.

Morgan, J. (1999). *When chickenheads come home to roost: My life as a hip hop feminist*. New York, NY: Simon & Schuster.

Morris, E.W. (2007). "Ladies" or "loudies"? Perceptions and experiences of Black girls in classrooms. *Youth and Society, 38*(4), 490–515.

Morris, M. (2016). *Pushout: The criminalization of Black Girls in Schools*. New York, NY: The New Press.

Muhammad, C. G., & Dixson, A. D. (2008). Black females in high school: A statistical educational profile. *The Negro Educational Review, 59*(3–4), 163–180.

Muhammad, G. E., & Haddix, M. (2016). Centering Black girls' literacies: A review of literature on the multiple ways of knowing Black girls. *English Education, 48*(4), 299–336.

Obama, M. (2018). *Becoming*. New York, NY: Crown Publishing Group.

Sealey-Ruiz, Y. (2007). Rising above reality: The voices of reentry Black mothers and their daughters. *Journal of Negro Education, 76*(2), 141–153.

Sears, S. D. (2010). *The negotiation of power and identity within the Girls Empowerment Project*. Albany: SUNY Press.

Steffans, K. (2005). *Confessions of a video vixen*. New York, NY: Harper Collins.

Index

Made in the USA
Coppell, TX
15 July 2023

19203382R00132